The Power of the Mind

The Power of the Mind

Healing through Hypnosis and Regression

JOE KEETON
with
SIMON PETHERICK

ROBERT HALE · LONDON

© *Joe Keeton and Simon Petherick 1988*
First published in Great Britain 1988

Robert Hale Limited
Clerkenwell House
Clerkenwell Green
London EC1R 0HT

British Library Cataloguing in Publications Data

Keeton, Joe
 The power of the mind : healing through
 hypnosis and regression.
 1. Hypnotism — Therapeutic use
 I. Title   II. Petherick, Simon
 615.8′512   RC495

 ISBN 0-7090-3278-1

Photoset in Ehrhardt in North Wales by
Derek Doyle & Associates, Mold, Clwyd.
Printed in Great Britain by
St Edmundsbury Press Ltd, Bury St Edmunds, Suffolk.
Bound by WBC Bookbinders Limited.

Contents

I would like to dedicate this book to Herbert Spencer (1820–1903) who said:

There is a principle which is a bar against all information, which is proof against all argument and which cannot fail to keep a man in everlasting ignorance. That principle is condemnation before investigation.

Author's Preface

This book is the result of a lifetime of doubting dogma. It is not autobiography, it is not scientific treatise, it is my attempt to tell of what I know.

I have never in my life been able to accept as truth any explanation that did not satisfy me. This caused me problems from an early age: expulsion from schools, condemnation from my elders. Later in life, once I had begun to enquire about the human brain, this attitude of mine – call it stubbornness if you will – left me with questions about all the theories of psychology, psychiatry and evolution that I read about. During the war I wondered at the way men coped with pain in such different ways, and I began to ask myself what more could be achieved if we understood the reasons behind those differences.

The questions grew. I wanted to know why animals could relax and yet stay alert, why humans could sleep through traffic noise but wake up at the sound of something unusual. I wanted to know why some people suffered more than others from the same sickness, and why some people remained sick no matter how many pills they took. Above all, I wanted to know why no one could answer my questions.

My search for knowledge ran concurrently with my work in hypnosis. I had been aware of my ability to induce the hypnotic state since an early age, but it was the encouragement of local doctors who recognized my role in helping people treat their own pain which persuaded me to become a professional hypnotherapist. Now I treat people regularly and with great success, by showing them how to unlock their own powers of self-healing. I work alongside the medical profession, treating those cases where modern medicine draws a blank: stress, cancer, arthritis, and many other ailments which *can* be healed by the mind. This I have proved, time and time again, under the most stringent conditions.

7

And yet the questions remain. What is this phenomenon we know as past-life regression which so frequently emerges under hypnosis? How many more self-healing abilities are you and I repressing beneath our twentieth-century outlook? For the moment, I offer this book as a document of what I have discovered to date. But it is time that hypnosis, hypnotherapy and hypnotic regression were taken out of the occult and accepted as a major new area for scientific study; for if there is one message I would like to spread, it is this: when we can see close-up photographs of the rings of Saturn, taken from a few thousand miles from the planet, it is a crime that we still cannot tell what is a few centimetres under our own skulls.

Finally, my thanks to everyone who helped with this book: those who made it possible and Simon Petherick who made it readable.

JK

Foreword by Professor Hugh Freeman

Nearly ten years ago, I first heard of the work of Joe Keeton through one of the medical journals. As a psychiatrist, it had always seemed to me very unfortunate that the possible value of hypnosis in both diagnosis and treatment had never been fully investigated. Psychiatric disorder is so common and often so difficult to treat that the potential contribution of hypnosis surely cannot be ignored. Yet I had never had the opportunity to learn this skill, and it has not become a regular part of psychiatric training since then. Nor has much been learnt as to what hypnosis is – except that it is clearly different from sleep.

When I had the chance to experience Joe Keeton's work, as I have since done on many occasions, I found that the ideas which I, as a professional in mental health, had held about hypnosis were mostly wrong. I had not realised that it requires active co-operation by the subject, that it does not withdraw the subject from awareness of his current situation, and that the will of the subject to control his own actions remains intact all the time. Many more people might be willing to accept the help that hypnosis can offer if these things were more widely understood.

Though sceptical at first about age regression, I was increasingly impressed by examples of it that I observed myself – particularly when my wife experienced it. Sigmund Freud abandoned hypnosis early in his career, because he believed it to be a short cut which would leave early emotional problems unsolved. No more than a handful of people will ever have the opportunity to undergo psychoanalysis – even if that should be the most effective approach – yet the alternative of hypnotic age-regression has never really been evaluated. I believe that the evidence offered by Joe Keeton and other reputable

9

hypnotherapists is more than enough to justify a major research effort to try and establish just how much can be achieved by this method.

When regression to previous existences was mentioned, I was even more sceptical – as most people are. However, again an experience my wife had led me to feel that this is at least a phenomenon which needs further examination. Certainly, personal observation of these cases is enough to make one conclude that wholesale dismissal of the paranormal is a form of unjustified dogmatism.

Not everyone can experience hypnosis, and those who can enter a deep trance are perhaps a minority. By no means all disorders, whether physical or psychiatric, can be helped by hypnotic treatment. But the evidence accumulated from Joe Keeton's many years of practice and study should be enough to convince most reasonable people that this is an aspect of the human mind which cannot be ignored.

Hugh Freeman
Consultant Psychiatrist,
University of Manchester School of Medicine

1 The Story of Ray Bryant

'I want you to go drifting back through time, further back through time, drifting …

'You're looking for a set of memories. It could be anybody, it could be anywhere, it could be anytime, but you're looking for a set of memories. You're looking for a set of memories.

'Some people say it's like going through a long, dark tunnel, but all tunnels come out into the daylight, and when you come out into the daylight you'll see where you are and you'll know your name. You'll know everything that's happened to you. So keep drifting back, looking for those memories …

'You're looking for memories, and they are memories of things that have happened to you. They have actually happened to you but they happened in times before you were born. You have not yet been born.

'So keep drifting back, keep drifting back, keep drifting back until you can see where you are. Can you see anything?'

Ray Bryant is about to begin a journey into the past. It is a journey with which he is familiar, for he has made it many times now, but there is no knowing where it may take him. All he can say is that he will once again experience a life before his own. He will relive the memories of the dead.

'I want you to go back, right back to times before you were born. Back in time. Bring out those memories.'

The room is silent. There is a sense of expectation, a tense, charged atmosphere amongst the observers. Ray lies in the chair, his eyes closed, his body relaxed. Everybody strains to hear the first word, to see the first movement. All eyes are on him.

'Back to a time before you were born. Go back to any set of memories from a time before you were born. You're there.

You're there now. *You're there now!'*

A flicker. His eyelids stir, his shoulders shift against the back of the chair. There's a sign of life about his face, an almost imperceptible working of the mouth. He is no longer slumped in that twilight world of deep relaxation.

'Hello. Who's there?'

A grunt from the person in the chair confirms what we all expected. Ray Bryant sits with eyes closed. He appears to be dreaming. But we know he is not.

Q: 'Hello. What's your name?'
A: 'Reuben.'
Q: 'Reuben what?'
A: 'Reuben … Reuben Sta … Reuben Sta … Sta …'

This is how we first came upon the life of Sergeant Reuben Stafford. Ray was struggling to produce a surname but could manage only the first three letters, a difficulty often encountered in these past-life regressions. In fact, this is how the search for a character always begins: a hesitant, stumbling affirmation of life, which gradually takes shape under patient questioning until a real person emerges.

Ray Bryant first encountered hypnosis and past-life regressions in 1981, when he came to research a series of features for the *Reading Evening Post*. Since that time he has returned again and again, to explore the memories that have been released from his unconscious. One of these sets of memories is particularly important, both to Ray and to the whole case for past-life regressions. It's important for the clarity with which Ray is able to recall the life of Sergeant Reuben Stafford. It's important for the consistency of those recollections. But its real importance lies in one special fact.

Sergeant Reuben Stafford really lived. We have found his Crimean War record. We have found his death certificate. We have uncovered a wealth of verifiable historical detail about the life of this nineteenth-century soldier, *none of which was shown to*

Ray until his own regression experiences confirmed the facts.

From further questions we established that Reuben Stafford was born in Brighthelmstone (now Brighton), Sussex, in the 1820s and moved to Ormskirk, Lancashire, when he was very young. Most of his life was spent as a soldier in the 47th Regiment of Foot. He reached the rank of sergeant, saw service in the Crimea and was married to a woman called Mary.

Q:　'I want you to go back to the year 1855. It is the year 1855. Bring out any memories you have of the year 1855. 'You there! What's your name and rank!'
A:　'Stafford, Sergeant.'
Q:　'Direct me to the barracks office, Sergeant.'
A:　'Sir ... Between the towers, sir ... through the gate ... on the right ...'

From exchanges like this, we began to build up a picture of the man whose memories were locked within Ray's subconscious. In this case, however, we were helped by a remarkable stroke of luck. Andrew Selby, one of the main researchers from the London group, was investigating another regressee's memories in the Record Office at Kew when he saw a book listing all the casualties in the Crimean War. We were still none the wiser about Reuben's surname at this point; he could get no further than 'Sta ...'. Andrew Selby began to look through the Crimea records, and on one page he found: 'Sgt Reuben Stafford, slight wound left hand. Battle of the Quarries. 7th of June 1855.' With this information he was able to obtain the entire army record of Sergeant Reuben Stafford. At the next session Ray, quite unaware of this development, took the chair as usual.

Q:　'Go back to any time before you were born when any of the following words meant anything to you: London, Liverpool, Glasgow, Manchester, Sheffield, Plymouth, Cambridge, Sutton, Newcastle, Stafford ...'

At this point, Ray stiffened and immediately resumed the

character of Sergeant Reuben Stafford. We had reached an exciting moment: we had established that Ray was regressing to a character named Reuben Stafford, and we had a full record of the army career of someone of the same name. Now we had to test to find out whether they were one and the same.

From the army records we knew that Stafford had served in Malta. I served in Malta myself during the last war, and so was able to set a few traps. Ray, by the way, had never been to any of the countries that border the Mediterranean.

Q: 'Go to any time when you were in the Strada Stretta.'

To this there was absolutely no response. I tried with an alternative:

Q: 'Go to any time when you were in the Gut.'
A: [loud, hearty chuckles]
Q: 'Hi there, Sergeant. What are you doing?'
A: [more laughter]: 'Don't think much on it.'
Q: 'What?'
A: 'I wouldn't have one of they wenches. Good lord!'
Q: 'What are you doing?'
A: 'Looking at a whore. God!'
Q: 'Some people must think they're all right.'
A: [more laughter]: 'Aye, pretty desperate.'
Q: 'Are you desperate, lad?'
A: 'Not that desperate yet. God, what a stink. Nowt here.'
Q: 'What do you think about the Gut?'
A: 'Too many steps and the ugliest set of bitches you can find anywhere.'

The Strada Stretta in Malta is known to most servicemen who have served on the island as 'the Gut'. This is usually the only name they know it by, as it has been ever since the first Malta garrison settled. It is not so much a street as a great series of flights of steps from one end to the other, and contained all the brothels in Valetta, the capital of the island.

We took Reuben to the day his army records said he was wounded.

Q: 'Go back to the time Reuben Stafford was at the Quarries.'
A: [panting heavily, a hoarse straining of his lungs, he seems to be choking]: 'Keep up ... keep up ... rest ... wait for the order ... rest ... keep down ...'

Suddenly Ray clutched his left hand; he screamed and appeared to be in such pain that I sent him off to a deep sleep. We brought him forward a few hours and found him in the field hospital having the hand re-dressed.

Further sessions with Ray brought out some fascinating insights into the reality of nineteenth-century warfare:

Q: 'How far did you march before you made contact?'
A: 'Few miles.'
Q: 'If you had used your rifles, do you think you would have made it back safely?'
A: 'I don't know. Orders are to fix bayonets in case of contact.'
Q: 'That seems a bit daft. If you used your rifles, you could kill them from a longer range, couldn't you?'
A: 'They come at us from just over a little ridge. They were right there in front of us, looking at us, hardly a rifle's length away.'
Q: 'Were they armed?'
A: 'Aye.'
Q: 'So you had to be quick?'
A: 'Too quick for 'em.'
Q: 'How old were they?'
A: 'Just chaps like us.'
Q: 'What colour uniforms are the Russians wearing?'
A: 'Grey. The grey ghosts. Just come and go. They know the country. Grey's the colour of the rock.'

Of course, one thing we never forgot was Ray's profession. As a journalist with many years' experience, he's had the opportunity to research into countless different subjects. He's written stories on almost every subject under the sun, and he's interviewed hundreds of subjects on a wide range of topics.

In other words, Ray must have an enormous amount of factual information stored in his subconscious, a great deal of which his conscious mind is unaware of. He might have some knowledge of the Crimea, even though there is no trace of his ever having written or researched anything on the subject throughout his career. For this reason we subjected his case to a more rigorous cross-examination than usual. At every session he attended he was switched backwards and forwards through the life of Reuben at very short intervals, never left on one particular day for more than a few minutes, and even tricked by questions about Ray's own life. Throughout such ordeals he never made a slip.

For example, we put some technical questions to him:

Q: 'What rifles are you using at the moment?'
A: 'The Enfield.'
Q: 'Magazine or single?'
A: 'Single shot.'
Q: 'How often do the Enfields jam?'
A: 'Not all that often.'
Q: 'Don't any of the rifles jam, then?'
A: 'Brownings. But we don't have the Brownings.'

Ray Bryant has precious little knowledge of firearms, or the army in general. He has never expressed any interest in the armed forces before, and obviously knows little about the army way of life. We knew Reuben received four campaign ribbons, but Ray seemed to disagree under questioning:

Q: 'Do you have any medals, Sergeant?'
A: 'Aye, three.'

Q: 'Only three? Are you sure?'
A: 'Aye.'
Q: 'But we've been told you have four.'
A: 'Oh, that Turkish thing. That's not a medal, it weren't given by the Queen.'

He was in fact referring to an award from the Turks of a campaign medal, which was the fourth medal mentioned in the records. Next we tested his drill:

Q: 'Go back to a time when you're giving recruits close order drill.'
A: 'Atten-shun! Straighten that line!'
Q: 'All right, Sergeant, I'll take over now. Atten-shun! Move to the right in threes. March. [Here Ray's face was puzzled.] What's the matter, Sergeant? Something wrong with my drill?'
A: 'In tandem, sir. Should be in tandem.'

He was quite correct. At the time of the Crimean War, the British Army was drilled in pairs, not in threes. Other remarkable details which Ray produced concerned his paydays and the days of his promotion to corporal and sergeant. No matter how much we tried to confuse him by throwing odd dates and events at him, he would invariably name the correct day of the correct month and would also tell us how much he received. Again, his army record confirmed those amounts.

There was a moving episode when we sent Ray back to the time when Reuben's ship was docking in Britain after the war:

Q: 'Hello, Reuben. Where've you been?'
A: 'Crimea.'
Q: 'How was it?'
A: 'Awful. This is what I wanted. I didn't think I was coming back. I'm going home now. Home to Ormskirk.'
Q: 'How long since you've seen your wife?'

A: 'Two year. And t'lad. He's about eighteen months now. [He begins to weep.] I never seen him yet.'

Q: 'Any others with you, Reuben?'

A: 'Andy Hudson.'

Q: 'What rank is he?'

A: 'Private.'

Q: 'Was he wounded?'

A: 'Aye, in the side. Great hole in the side.'

Q: 'Did you know J.H. Lowndes?'

A: 'Aye, Captain Lowndes. He was Company Commander.'

Q: 'What do you think of him, Sergeant?'

A: 'He's quite a character.'

Q: 'What's happened to him?'

A: 'Wounded.'

Q: 'And Villiers?'

A: 'Colonel Villiers. Don't know.'

Q: 'What about Beetson?'

A: 'Aye, I know Beetson. He were all right. Bit morbid, always moaning. Nothing right for him.'

Q: 'What about the name Kelly?'

A: 'Aye. All Kelly lads got wounded. I think one of them died.'

Q: 'How many Kellys were there?'

A: 'I knew three.'

Every detail was correct.

Ray has also been featured on a series of television programmes produced by Arthur C. Clarke, where he was taken blindfold into the museum of the Lancashire Regiment. The blindfold was removed only after he was seated in a position where he could see very little of anything in the museum. Colonel Richard Bird, the officer in charge of the museum at Fulwood Barracks, Preston, had agreed to do all the questioning for the programme.

Colonel Bird picked a lesser-known battle of the Crimean War to test Ray, one which he knew the 47th had led. Reuben described the river-crossing and the bombardment by the Russian guns situated on the hills overlooking the river, and named many of the casualties, all to Colonel Bird's satisfaction. He was asked what items the regiment captured.

A: 'Some drums and flags and things.'
Q: 'What are the drums like?'
A: 'Shiny, made o' brass or something like that.'
Q: 'Anything on them?'
A: 'Aye sir, some o' them ... like them things you see in church.'

Indeed, the embossed spread eagles which decorated the body of the drums do resemble the eagles on the lecterns in some churches.

The life of Reuben Stafford was not all hardship, and there were many moments of light relief during the sessions we conducted with Ray:

Q: 'Go to any time in the life of Reuben Stafford when he was looking in a mirror or saw his full reflection in something.' [Ray takes on a proud, rather vain stance.]
Q: 'What are you looking at? Going out tonight or something?'
A: 'Aye.'
Q: 'Who are you going with?'
A: 'Mary. [Smiles.] Reckon she'll like that ... She'll like me. I'm handsome fellow.'
Q: 'Have you got a moustache?'
A: 'Aye. I'm handsome corporal.'

Sadly, Reuben's life took a downward turn. By sending him back to different periods, we discovered he ended up as a lighterman on the Thames after his discharge from the army. He was living at Gravesend, bronchitic from the cold, lack of food and poor clothing of the Crimea. He had been widowed and was obviously very miserable. He had one son, an architect, whom he seldom saw. After extensive checking, Marguerite Selby, another researcher, found a death certificate for Reuben Stafford, dated April 1879: 'Reuben Stafford. Violent suffocation by drowning. How caused not proved. Milwall dock found dead on 2nd April, 1879.'

Ray agreed, after considerable thought, to be taken back to that day, to a few minutes before the death by drowning of Reuben Stafford. At this stage we had not told Ray the details of the death certificate, so he was ignorant of the way Reuben had died. We found him standing on the dockside in Milwall. Within a few minutes he was choking and gasping, obviously drowning.

After he was roused, Ray was shown the certificate, and for the very first time he was allowed to examine the copies of the army record sheets. He was silent for some time, and then said: 'At least he ended his misery and found peace.'

But it is not just Reuben Stafford whose memories live on in the unconscious mind of Ray Bryant. When he is hypnotized, Ray also regresses to other characters from the past. We have found an eighteenth-century coachman named Wilfred Anderton:

Q: 'Hello there. What's your name?'
A: 'Wilfred.'
Q: 'Where are you going?'
A: 'I going Bath.'
Q: 'How long does that take?'
A: 'Starts out in afternoon. We'm down there next morning.'
Q: 'Where do you change the horses?'
A: 'Oxford.'
Q: 'Where do you leave from?'
A: 'The Bar in Fleet Street.'
Q: 'Where do you leave London?'
A: 'Hounslow.'
Q: 'How do you get to Hounslow?'
A: 'There's only one bloody road out of London.'
Q: 'Where do you stay in Bath?'

A: 'The Cock.'
Q: 'Where's that?'
A: 'Near the Pump Room.'
Q: 'Have you been there?'
A: 'No, it's for nobs ... dandies.'
Q: 'Have you always done this?'
A: 'Aye.'
Q: 'You must be healthy.'
A: 'Not too much. Got wheezes.'
Q: 'What age did you start?'
A: 'Fourteen or fifteen.'
Q: 'Which companies have you worked for?'
A: 'Cobb. Tennyson.'
Q: 'How's the wife?'
A: 'I don't know. I ain't seen her in a year or so.'
Q: 'How's she living?'
A: 'Her's got her money.'
Q: 'How?'
A: 'Her takes in washing.'
Q: 'Are you religious?'
A: 'I goes careful. Tries not to offend 'im.'

Wilfred is a carefree, amusing character, quite in contrast to another of Ray's regressions, that of a seventeenth-century governess called Elizabeth:

Q: 'I want you to go back to fifteen years before the birth of Wilfred. Hello there, what's your name?'
A: 'My name is Elizabeth.'
Q: 'What are you doing?'
A: 'I'm walking with Jack. He's my charge.'
Q: 'How old is he?'
A: 'He's eight. I'm his governess.'
Q: 'Is he well-behaved?'
A: 'He's quite correct.'
Q: 'What do you do with him?'

A: 'I teach him proper behaviour.'
Q: 'How do you punish him when he's naughty?'
A: 'I correct him. I speak sternly with him.'
Q: 'What does his father do?'
A: 'He is at Court.'
Q: 'Whose Court?'
A: 'King William.'
Q: 'Has the King got a Queen?'
A: 'Mary.'
Q: 'Have you been with the family long?'
A: 'I have been in my position for ten years. I am in my seventieth year. I have seen many great families, many great houses. I have been to the palace of Whitehall.'
Q: 'What are the names of some of the families?'
A: 'The Harcourts.'
Q: 'Where was their family seat?'
A: 'Huntingdon.'
Q: 'Go back to the age of twenty. The memories of Elizabeth at the age of twenty. Hello, how are you?'
A: 'Quite well, thank you.'
Q: 'Where are you living?'
A: 'The Hall.'
Q: 'Which Hall?'
A: 'Petersfield.'
Q: 'What's the family called?'
A: 'Egerton.'
Q: 'What position do you hold?'
A: 'House-parlourmaid.'
Q: 'Do you have a boyfriend?'
A: 'Don't … no …'
Q: 'Are you all right?'
A: 'Quite well.'
Q: 'Would you like a boyfriend?'
A: '*No!*'
Q: 'Why not?'
A: 'I am not permitted.'

Q: 'Ah. Have you ever had one?'
A: 'At twenty-five I may marry.'

Reuben, Wilfred, Elizabeth ... are the memories of these people really preserved in the mind of a journalist named Ray Bryant? It is uncanny to watch Ray as he is switched from one character to another in a gruelling session, often concentrating for hours at a time. From the broad Lancashire accent of Reuben to the prim, rather pompous tones of Elizabeth and the rich West Country drawl of Wilfred – is he just a very good actor, with a script which is accurate down to the tiniest detail? If so, he has worked in the wrong profession all his life. No, such a sustained performance under such conditions would not be expected of the most experienced performer. But how *can* he know the very day when Sergeant Reuben Stafford received his wages, and how *can* he tell us the exact sum he received?

The experiences of Ray Bryant under hypnosis have told us many things over the years. They have introduced into our lives the stories of individuals who are now long dead, whose memories, emotions and thoughts can be as moving as those of a living person. They have given us a glimpse of life as it has been lived over the centuries, with its hardships, its moments of happiness, its griefs, its joys. But most of all, they have made us question our own mortality.

'I want you to go back ...'

With these words, all the mysteries and the enigmas of hypnosis begin. It is time we understood them.

2   The Hidden Mind

The unconscious
The human brain has been investigated by philosophers and
scientists for centuries. They have dissected, probed, examined,
discussed, weighed and tested it; they have subjected it to closer
scrutiny than perhaps any other organ of the body. Yet despite
these efforts, we are still far from any proper definition of what
we call 'the mind' – the function, both conscious and
unconscious, which is at the very centre of all we know to be
human.

People like Ray Bryant, who have undergone hypnotic
regression to reach back to past lives, are aware that the mind
contains mysteries far greater than they ever imagined. They
know that within the unconscious, the hidden mind, there is a
source of knowledge, and possibly power, that is only just
beginning to be tapped.

The conscious and the unconscious: two quite separate
components of the mind. But they are by no means equal.
Scientific tests reveal that the conscious mind – the part which
responds to external stimuli and which delivers commands to
the body – makes up only one eleventh of the mind. The
unconscious, a full ten-elevenths of the whole, is by far the
dominating element. In other words, we are able to think and
operate every day on a fraction of our capacity, like a
high-powered engine forever running in low gear.

The body's automatic reflexes and safety circuits are kept
within the unconscious. It is this which operates 'when we are
not thinking', when our conscious minds are concerned with
something else. If we become frightened, our heart-beat
increases, stimulating the production of adrenalin to give us
extra strength for 'flight or fight'; this is not a process set into

25

motion deliberately by the conscious mind.

We may not understand this hidden power within us, but we can observe its peculiar effect. The next time you go to what you expect to be a large and noisy party, take a tape-recorder and make sure it is recording when the party is in full swing. When you play it back, you'll be surprised to hear only a loud hubbub from which it is impossible to pick out any one voice. Yet while you were there, you were talking to people, having a conversation and clearly hearing people's responses. It is the conscious mind in such a situation which lets you concentrate only on the person or persons you wish to hear; the unconscious, like the tape, records everything.

Herein lie the mystery and the wonder which are the subject of this book. The unconscious stores everything it experiences. No matter how trivial the information, it is just waiting to be recalled from memory. The cases of hypnotic regression described later provide irrefutable evidence for this extra-ordinary ability. For if we can gain access to the material contained in the unconscious, we can revolutionize the very concept of memory.

For example, we might want to remember the telephone number of a friend. His number is written down in an address book, which we can visualize. By calling on our unconscious memory, we can also visualize exactly where the book is now, and what is written on each page. (Remember, we wrote every entry in that book, so our unconscious contains the memories of each entry as we made it.) In other words, we can remember something we had 'forgotten'. As we will show later, this is not as preposterous as it may sound: it is a technique used by those who have learned how to gain access to the unconscious.

There is nothing mysterious about using powers that are already within us. In the chapter on physical healing, we will show how many people have conquered illnesses previously diagnosed as incurable, just as animals do and just as we used to before we became so sophisticated. The unconscious could be the key to a new age of health, and a way out from much of the oppressive currency of modern medical drugs.

The optic nerves, like photographic film, are sensitive to light energy and are constantly reacting to external stimuli around us. Every day we 'see' our world as it is translated into a visual image in our conscious mind. The pictures we 'see' are then stored away in the unconscious, just as any other kind of information that is not of immediate use to the conscious mind is recorded. And in the same way as a projector will show a picture from a slide onto a screen, our unconscious visual memory can project a scene, perhaps from many years ago, as clearly as if we were 'seeing' it now.

This normally occurs when we are sleeping and dreaming, although of course everyone has experienced those curious flashes of visual memory which appear unbidden and unexpected. Closed eyelids are like a cinema screen, showing us only memories from the past, but visual memories in our waking state can be superimposed on everyday life: a rose can be conjured up whilst sitting at an office desk, a house from childhood recalled in precise detail many years later.

Visual memories such as these probably explain most claims for ghostly sightings. One volunteer at our sessions had 'seen' a ghost with no legs. Under hypnosis, he revealed that at the time he had been thinking of a colleague sitting at his desk. Superimposed on his line of vision, this visual memory appeared as a legless apparition! A person from one's own life, a person from a character drama or film on television: either could produce a very authentic-looking 'ghost' in the right circumstances.

The implications are dramatic: if visual memory functions as effectively as factual memory, how much is waiting to be discovered within the memory banks of the unconscious? A man of fifty is capable of recalling everything from his tenth year, his fifth year, his first year, and is capable of 'seeing' his experiences again just as he first saw them.

But he can, if he wants, see more.

Many years of investigation have shown me that the factual and visual memory-banks of our unconscious minds may contain the details of more than just our own lives. I say 'may' because I am not in the business of making broad claims or sweeping generalizations and, as later chapters show, I am keen to assess every explanation for the phenomenon we call hypnotic regression. Nevertheless, I am sure no reader could finish this book and still feel confident that he 'knows his own mind'.

Before we go on to study these cases of regression, however, it is useful to remember the context within which we are working.

'The past,' said L.P. Hartley, 'is a foreign country: they do things differently there.' True enough, but not so foreign, and not so different, that we may not gain access to it. Take a walk through any graveyard and you will see how many of our ancestors achieved the biblical standard of three score years and ten. Ten lifetimes therefore will take us back to the thirteenth century; twenty to the sixth century. In fact, it is only approximately twenty-eight lifetimes which separate us from the life of Jesus Christ. Anyone today who is a hundred years old was alive at the time of the first incandescent gas mantle, the first electric tramcar, the fall of Khartoum, the Ripper murders. They saw the first television receivers, telephones, wireless sets, underground railways, and have lived through dozens of wars.

In other words, what gives us a greater sense of perspective is not chronology but the links between ourselves and the past.

History is also transmitted by word of mouth, as folklore and legend within families and cultures. Stories are passed down from generation to generation, and a child might hear of the exploits of a great-great-great-grandfather as though he were still alive. Of course, the stories become distorted with the retelling, but remember that, in theory, it would be possible for a story to have been told only twenty-eight times for it to be passed down from the first century to the present day. By this method the past is kept alive, and we maintain our links, however tenuous, with events from before our time.

History, too, is not a fixed, unchanging discipline but is as contingent as the present upon human interpretation. The accounts that we read of the past are riddled with distortion and bias, as succeeding generations attempt to impose their own stamp upon their times. The Tudors rewrote the history of Edward IV, the Germans rewrote the history of the Jews, the *Anglo-Saxon Chronicle* presents a picture of eighth-century England which is as 'true' as we decide.

Similarly, the recording of information is by no means scientific. Even today, many individuals find themselves left off the census figures: how much more inaccurate must earlier census returns have been? Public records of births and deaths can occasionally be wrong on dates, and deliberate falsification of information can preserve inaccuracy for posterity.

Consider what happens when we research our family tree. We start with the birth certificates of our parents, grandparents and so on, in the national register of births, marriages and deaths. Beyond this, we resort to the parish records. But what if we want to go further? How far *can* we research back, before all sources of information dry up? And even if we could research back as far as we wanted, how could we keep control of the mushrooming numbers involved: first two parents, then four grandparents, eight great-grandparents, sixteen great-great-grandparents, thirty-two great-great-great-grandparents, sixty-four great-great-great-great-grandparents. And what of cousins, uncles, aunts? We could soon get back to the time when the entire population of the world was insufficient to have been the ancestors of any one person.

Think of the distortions that would be bound to occur within such a family tree! But our sense of history, our feeling for the separation between past and present, is also a casualty of this method and cannot be so straightforward, so linear, as the history books would have it. The past is within us now, within the genetically inherited cells which make up our bodies; the fact of having ancestors presupposes continuity and permanence. The past is a kaleidoscope of events, reports, impressions, characters, sights and colours, all of which are passed down on paper, by word of mouth and by memory. The past is, in fact, anything but secure, and it is up to us to reclaim it.

The cases which follow of past-life regression go some way towards bridging that invisible gap between now and then. They could offer proof that, far from being stranded in our own time, we are joined with everything that has ever happened and with everyone who has ever lived.

The mechanics of hypnosis

There is so much nonsense talked about hypnosis that it is probably wisest to begin by destroying a few myths.

All hypnosis is self-hypnosis. No one can be induced into a hypnotic state against his or her will, and the idea that a weak mind is taken over by a stronger, more manipulative mind is simply not true. Hypnotists do not possess the power to control other people's minds; they just point the way to a deep state of relaxation which is available to everyone. And the final myth to be disposed of is this: under hypnosis, you do not say things you do not believe; you merely dispense with the inhibitions which normally prevent your saying what you feel. But you are always in full control of what you say, and if you do not want to reveal your most intimate secrets, you won't.

There are various states of the mind which are often considered to be forms of hypnosis, particularly suggestion and meditation. But, unlike true – or deep – hypnosis, these states operate only on the conscious level; they do not reach down into the unconscious mind.

Suggestion is the lightest state and strictly speaking is not an altered state of consciousness at all. It is the state which was used so much in the past by doctors when prescribing a placebo. Patients would swallow a sugar-coated pill which contained no drugs, in the belief that it was a highly effective medicine. Usually they were cured of their ailment, but only because they believed in the 'cure'. This kind of suggestion operates throughout our daily lives. In the supermarket, certain goods are placed in optimum selling positions, so that those with the highest profit margin are sold first. We call this 'impulse buying' but forget that the impulse was planted in us first. Bottles are designed to look bigger and better, packages produced which seem more attractive than others. This is all deliberate suggestion, which of course operates most effectively in advertising.

If you are the sort of person who always leaves a supermarket with only the goods you went in for, you can proudly boast that you are not a suggestive type. However, you will probably be an excellent subject for hypnosis, because it is the suggestive type who have most difficulty in achieving this deep state of relaxation.

Successful practitioners of yoga and transcendental meditation report feeling relaxed after a session, and there is no reason to doubt them. But it does appear that this state does not last long and that all too soon they are back to the normal stress of modern living. The chapter on physical therapy shows the huge difference between conscious and unconscious forms of relaxation, and those who do succeed in meditating usually find difficulty with true hypnosis because, again, true hypnosis works on the unconscious mind.

True hypnosis dispenses with these superficial notions. In the real, deep state of hypnosis, the body is relaxed but the mind is alert. Think of a dog coming into a room. It will walk across to where it wants to sit, lie down and immediately seem to have entered a state of deep sleep. Yet it will be aware of sounds around it long before we humans are, and will snap out of its sleep the moment it hears anything unusual.

This is the kind of relaxation that can be achieved under hypnosis. It is no miracle, it involves no trickery, but it releases us from our self-imposed limitations. In the times when we were hunters, we had the same ability to relax, and relied upon our unconscious minds to watch over us while we rested. Hypnosis has been proved to bring about a heightened sense of hearing, and even people with hearing difficulties experience an improvement. While we are hypnotized, we recover the powers which, over the centuries, ensured our survival.

Evolution is described as the survival of the fittest: those creatures which adapted successfully to their environment survived, and those which failed to improve on their weaknesses became extinct. It is a cruel process, conducted on an arbitrary basis by the method of genetic inheritance. The shape of our bodies is a witness to this haphazard but logical progression; we are living proof of the value of change.

But we are still evolving. We may have achieved a physique which is suitable for our surroundings, but we are vulnerable to disease, a hostage to the stresses of society. Hypnosis offers us the chance to harness all the strengths we have ever possessed and to use them in the fight for survival.

Look around our world: are we winning the fight or losing it?

The sessions I conduct, many of which are described in this book, begin the same way. Those who wish to undergo hypnosis gather in a room, an ordinary room with no special lighting or furniture. A chair is allocated, and the first subject sits down. I speak in a clear, unhurried tone, guiding the person down into a state of deep relaxation. Sometimes this can happen immediately; sometimes it takes a few minutes. If the person wants to discover that state of relaxation and is not excessively nervous or distracted, he will reach it.

With eyes closed, but always fully aware of his surroundings, the subject will respond as he wishes to any questions I may ask. He may refuse to speak about something, and if so I simply move on to a new topic. I may ask him to remember times when he was younger and, calling on his unconscious memory, he will see, hear and feel again just as he did then. A grown man may stamp his feet and yell like a child, an elderly woman may smile at the recollection of her mother's face – if I ask them to remember, then it is in their power to do so, absolutely. And remember, everything is taped so we may share in the experience afterwards.

For those who wish to experience it, another past is also waiting. I will ask a subject to go back to times before he was born; then I, and everyone else in the room, must wait. Not everyone can do so. Many people retain 'blocks' within their unconscious minds, enforced areas of forgetfulness which protect them from an unpleasant memory and which stop them from going beyond that point. In the chapter on psychological healing we will examine this self-defence mechanism in detail and show how, by clearing these blocks, we can rid ourselves of unnecessary trauma.

Clearing the blocks can take time, sometimes demanding many sessions, but eventually they will be cleared. The road then lies open to the extraordinary phenomenon known as hypnotic regression. Everyone in the room will have the opportunity to question the person whose memories have been recalled by the subject in the chair. Gradually, often over many sessions, we will begin to build up a picture of this person and, as was shown in Chapter 1, come to know them as we would a friend.

True or false? Reality or fantasy? The next chapter will let you decide for yourself. But remember, the cases we are about to describe really happened, in a room just as I have described, and witnessed by changing groups of observers and participants. The tests we conducted were rigorous, sometimes resulting in a subject under hypnosis being questioned at speed by different people on different subjects for hours at a time. Facts were checked, false trails laid, tricks played and, as you will see, many cases of apparent past-life regression turn out to be the astonishing imagination of the unconscious mind at work.

But there remain the cases, and many are included here, where our cross-questioning draws a blank, leaving, it seems, only one possible explanation.

That we are talking to the dead.

3   Past-Life Regression

There is no lack of plausible explanations for what we are about to consider. The greater the mystery, it seems, the swifter the flow of theories, and the subject of past-life regression is perhaps one of the most beguiling mysteries of all. The idea of going back over one's own life and reliving events as they occurred: this is a difficult enough achievement to swallow. But to discover the lives of other people, people who now are dead, and to be able to go over the events of their lives in just the same way, to hear those people 'talk' again as once they might have done? To be able, now, to communicate with people from previous centuries: what kind of explanation can we find for that?

As this chapter will show, there *are* ways of understanding this phenomenon. Nothing can remain mysterious for ever, and if our knowledge is still limited, it is only a matter of time before experience and experiment fill it out. Meanwhile, we must be patient and methodical because, from what we have discovered to date, it seems we are about to reconstruct all our notions of the mind and mortality.

Verification procedures

Hypnosis is not an exact science with laws and regulations to follow, and memory is notoriously unreliable. Past-life regression combines the two, and we should insist on the most scrupulous methods of investigation. The memories of a subject's own life, which are often recalled with all the tears, laughter and anger of the original event, always appear utterly true to life. But as they occurred during the subject's own lifetime, they can always be checked against the facts and other people's recollections.

The memories of a past life are, however, more difficult to verify. We can begin with the more obvious methods. If someone appears to be regressing to the life of an ancient Egyptian, we would expect him to understand and respond only in the language of the time. If he speaks perfectly good English, he cannot be back in the memories of someone who had no knowledge of the English language. The following case demonstrates this quite clearly.

A young woman in her early twenties came to one of my regression groups and proved to be an excellent subject for hypnosis. I began to take her back over her own life, and she responded by recalling vividly each moment to which she was taken. Then, suddenly, she stopped. It was obvious that she no longer understood our questions, so we asked her mother if there had been anything wrong with the girl at the age we had reached. She told us that her daughter had been brought up in Brazil and had spoken no English until the age of seventeen. Now, this fact had not been mentioned before, and none of us had even known the woman had grown up in Brazil; her English now was perfect. After a short lesson in Portuguese, we took the woman back to that same point and then addressed her in her native language. She understood immediately and continued to go back over the events of her childhood.

That young woman was experiencing the events of her life all over again; if she had not been, she would have been able to understand our English throughout the process of recall.

Language is a key factor in establishing the validity of a regression. A subject must be able to speak the language of the character to whom he or she has regressed, *exactly as that character would have spoken it*. For example, a Dutch woman who has lived in Britain for over twenty-five years came to one of our sessions. Her friends back home in the Netherlands always told her that she now spoke Dutch with an English accent. But when they heard the tape of her regression back to the times before her departure from the Netherlands, they were amazed to hear her speaking just like a native again.

Similarly a past-life regression should bring about a change in the speaking patterns of the subject. The accent will probably be different, but also the syntax will most likely have altered. A middle-aged bank manager from Hampshire will not sound the same, or use the same modes of speech, as a nineteenth-century Mancunian labourer, and under hypnosis a true regression will bring out such changes. If a subject fails to understand slang expressions from the period to which he or she is claiming to be regressing, then again some doubt must be cast.

Above all, it is very important to remain critical and to resist the temptation to 'interpret' what someone says under hypnosis. We always try to avoid leading questions, even where this leads to protracted questioning or dead ends. For example, without hypnosis, we once asked a woman what she remembered about September 1939.

'Oh,' came the immediate reply, 'I was twenty-one that month and I had a beautiful blue dress for my party.'

Perhaps if we had slanted the question in a more obvious way, she would have recalled that World War II started that month! But people's memories are more often concerned with everyday matters, and it is only when they are prompted that they start to look beyond their personal circumstances. In regression, how- ever, we cannot prompt, or we will quite fairly be accused of manipulation. This difficulty is compounded when dealing with memories from times when news was not as readily available as it is today. An eighteenth-century farmer would have known little of national significance, and the distribution of news would have incorporated inaccuracies and distortion. So we must be patient.

However difficult the task, there is always a way of conducting research on a past-life regression. It is often long and arduous, but as the case of Ray Bryant in Chapter 1 showed, it can repay the effort many times over. And as the following case shows, the truth will come out somehow.

A dental student volunteered for regression and was soon going back over events from her life. Later on in the session, she began to chatter away in a language which no one could understand. We suspected she might be regressing to a past life, and as the language sounded vaguely Germanic, one of the observers agreed to investigate all possible dialects of the Central European countries, ancient and modern. No progress was made, despite the research, until the student's mother heard a tape of her daughter's regression. She recognized the language immediately. It was the baby-language the girl used to babble away in as a child.

Fantasy and imagination

There are some people who hold that all past-life regressions are pure fantasy. If the fantasy happens to coincide with verifiable truth, then that is all it is: coincidence. It is impossible, these people say, for memories to live on; therefore, the only explanation must be that it is the imagination at work.

There is some truth in this theory. Think of the games you used to play as a child, where a back garden or a bedroom floor could become an enchanted, foreign country, peopled by knights, princesses, fairies, cowboys and others. Remember how real those games seemed, how powerful the dramas that were played out. That was imagination, but at such an age it could easily assume the same importance as reality.

Under hypnosis, an adult can rediscover the imaginative delights of the unconscious mind and can once again convince himself that fantasy is in fact reality. There is nothing deliberate or misleading in this; it is just that the imaginative capacity of the unconscious is far more powerful than we are used to in everyday life. Adults, too, have greater knowledge and experience than children, so when they come to fantasize in the relaxed atmosphere of hypnosis they can produce quite startlingly lifelike dramas.

It is, however, fairly easy to spot a fantasy at work. Take the young woman who claimed, under hypnosis, to be called Josephine. Unsurprisingly, she was sailing to France to see an emperor named Napoleon. We began to question her. Was the ship she was sailing on clinker- or carvel-built? She did not understand the question, and admittedly it was rather technical. Instead, we asked her to look over the side and tell us whether the planks overlapped or simply met one another. Back came her reply:

'It is not made of wood; it is all metal.'

We can be pretty certain that Napoleon preceded the first all-metal ship by a good few years!

Similarly, one session we held in the Midlands was attended by a local journalist. He had come to write a story on regression and ended up by regressing himself. He said his name was Brian Boru, the famous king of ancient Ireland, and the details he produced were marvellously lifelike and evocative. The session had, in fact, become quite fascinating until a journalist from another paper asked:

'If you wanted to go to England, how would you travel there?'

He replied immediately: 'Sure, I'd go to Shannon and fly.'

Such feats of imagination are common under hypnosis, but they are not intended to deceive; indeed, the person who produces them is usually astounded. It is always possible to identify them, however, even if it takes lengthy questioning. Many take their theme from Hollywood films or classic tales, and the following example shows just how realistic a performance they can produce.

An American woman in her twenties, on her first visit to one of my regression groups, gave us a tale straight out of Tennessee Williams. She said she was a girl living in the Everglades in the early nineteenth century. At one point she mentioned that her brother was in the army and visiting France with the American Expeditionary Force. We asked her if she had ever seen him in uniform, and she said she had. She was then put to a time when she was looking at him in his uniform, and asked to describe it. She gave a pretty accurate picture of a uniform of the period but did not describe the badge. We then told her the badge should contain stags and a crown, which in fact would be quite untrue. She accepted this and even described it as though she were seeing it herself. Her tale, fascinating as it was, was a fantasy.

In another regression, the same American woman told us she was being kept virtually a prisoner in the home of an uncle. She said she was being forced to sign papers at regular intervals, handing properties over to her uncle. We questioned her on this.

Q: 'Why does he not ask you to sign one giving him all at once?'
A: 'The King would not allow it.'
Q: 'Who is the King?'
A: 'Edward I.

That seems reasonable, doesn't it? Except that, if you were living in the time of Edward I, you would know him as King Edward – for who could tell he would be the first of many?

Sometimes the fantasies which people produce under hypnosis can be as entertaining as those for which no 'rational' explanation can be found. Just because they are fantasies, the powers of the unconscious which called them up are no less impressive for that, and everyone who has produced such a tale in one of our sessions has been amazed to find such creativity within themselves.

But the role of the imagination can always be identified by simple methods such as those used on the previous cases. It cannot be identified in the cases which follow. The lives that are recalled are not from the pages of some bestselling book, nor are they copied from some Hollywood film. They are real people, living ordinary, often uneventful lives, whose memories have somehow been preserved after their death. It is time, then, to discard the theory of fantasy, for it cannot explain what we know.

Parallel universes

In the 1920s the world of physics was shaken to its foundations by the development of a new theory. Called the quantum theory, it redefined the nature of matter and consequently revolutionized our understanding of the world. Essentially, it stated that the atomic world is far from comprehensible and rational. A sub-atomic particle such as the electron does not follow any path or route which can be pre-determined; it is, as far as we perceive it, thoroughly unstable and unpredictable. We have the equipment to identify an electron, to plot its position at any one moment, but we have absolutely no idea where it will be next. The same goes for all other sub-atomic particles, and for atoms: we cannot predict their movements with any confidence at all.

In other words, what seems to us a solid and reassuringly concrete world is in fact a hazy jumble of incomprehensible particles.

Now, as if this were not enough to shatter our complacency about the world and about ourselves, a new theory based on quantum physics was put forward by the physicist Hugh Everett in 1957. It was called the theory of parallel universes. For every movement of an atomic or sub-atomic particle, a multitude of different movements could have taken place, all equally unpredictable and arbitrary. And if each such movement was equally likely or unlikely, each must in fact have happened. So alongside our universe, the universe we see and experience every day, there must be an infinite number of parallel universes which are just as 'real' as our own, with observers as 'real' as we consider ourselves to be.

Crazy? It sounds so, of course, but then the quantum theory itself is shocking enough. And if the theory of parallel universes remains a possibility amongst physicists, we are certainly in no position to dispute it. But what I am trying to tell you in this book is shocking: people have experienced the lives of the dead. If we are to comprehend something as momentous as that, we must be prepared for the unusual.

So, somewhere, a world might exist where Hitler won the last war. Where the person you married decided to marry someone else. Where your favourite song was never sung. Could there be a link between us and these parallel universes? We cannot tell, but perhaps it may give us a clue as to why one woman, when regressed under hypnosis, insisted that Queen Victoria was on the throne as late as 1915. Consciously, she knew that Queen Victoria had died in 1901, but under hypnosis she could not be shaken from her belief that she was still alive fourteen years later.

The following case study could serve to illustrate several of the theories for hypnotic regression which we will deal with later. It could possibly be a case of cryptamnesia, where everything the mind has ever experienced or read is stored in the unconscious; it could be a case of reincarnation. But we will look at it here to see whether it casts any more light on the theory of parallel universes.

Ann Dowling originally came to our hypnotic regression sessions because of recurrent nightmares which, from early childhood, had always followed the same pattern. In one, she was sitting in a bare room, absolutely terrified; in another, she was in a dank, dirty basement with a rough-looking man who was threatening her with a knife. These nightmares were so frightening that her parents, and then her late husband, had to waken her to stop her screaming.

Under hypnosis, we found the key to her nightmares. Her first regression was to a little girl called Sarah Williams, living on the streets of Everton in the early 1800s. Her father had died, and instead of going into an orphanage she had run away from the authorities. Her mother had died giving birth to her, and as far as she knew she had no other relatives.

When we first found her, Sarah was sitting at home, cold, hungry and apprehensive. Night was falling, and her father had not returned from the docks, where he worked as a labourer. As the evening wore on, the little girl became more and more agitated, looking out of the window in the hope of catching sight of her father. Suddenly, she said a man was coming to the door. There was a pause, and she seemed to be listening to what he had to say. Then she broke down completely.

A: 'E ... e ... says me dad isn't comin' 'ome.'
Q: 'Who says that?'
A: 'E says 'is name's Johnson.'
Q: 'What exactly did he tell you?'

A: 'E ... said a 'orse done somethin' to me dad ... me dad isn't comin' 'ome an' I got to go wi' 'im ... a 'orse done somethin' terrible to me dad.'

She was asked whether any neighbours could help, and she said that a Mrs Vaughan lived next door. But she didn't want to go and see her; she would wait until her dad got home. Lonely and afraid, the poor girl was unable to comprehend a world without her father, the only person she was close to; the only person, it seemed, who cared for her.

A: 'E wouldn't leave me, e love me, e'll come 'ome, e loves me.'

It was a pitiful sight, and a very moving experience for everyone present. But Sarah's plight grew worse. We brought her forward twenty-four hours and found her still in the same room. The house, however, was practically bare of furniture, and she was hungry. We asked her what had happened to the furniture, and she said that Mrs Vaughan and the other neighbours had 'borrowed' it, but that her father would get it back when he came home. Not only had they stolen her furniture, they had obviously also not fed her.

With her father dead, Sarah was forced out onto the streets and for years survived on her wits, receiving charity occasionally but usually living on scraps of food and sleeping in whatever shelter she could find. Over a hundred hours of regression brought out the fascinating and sad details of her poverty-stricken life, and extraordinary information such as this, when we sent her to 12 July 1835:

Q: 'What are you doing today, Sarah?'
A: 'Do ... I gotta stay in, can't go out today.'
Q: 'Why not?'
A: 'It's them.'
Q: 'Who's them?'
A: 'Them Irish. They're mad, fighting all over the place.

They must've been 'avin' that 'oly water again.'
Q: 'It can't be that bad.'
A: 'It is. They've 'ad to fetch the soldiers out.'
Q: 'What day is it?'
A: 'It's Sunday. That's why they've 'ad the 'oly water.'

On that weekend in July 1835, the records show that there was serious rioting in the neighbourhood of Marybone, Tithebarn Street, Vauxhall Road and other parts of the town. The military were called out on 12 July. It was a Sunday.

Another time we put Sarah back to January 1839 and found her huddled in a ball, shivering and very frightened.

Q: 'What's the matter, Sarah?'
A: 'It's awful, blowin' roofs off and howlin'.'

On 6 January 1839 a hurricane descended on Liverpool and continued until the following afternoon, wreaking havoc with life and property.

Taken to 1848, Sarah produced this memorable piece of local gossip:

Q: 'Anything happening in Liverpool, Sarah?'
A: 'They're all talkin' about 'im.'
Q: 'Talking about who?'
A: ''im, Albert.'
Q: 'Who is Albert?'
A: ''im Queen's 'usband. She's mad, you know.'
Q: 'What makes you say that?'
A: 'Everybody knows it. He's been carryin' on wi' Mayor's wife. He keeps comin' to see 'er. 'E's 'ad to give 'er a cradle for t'babby.'

The records show that on 30 October 1848 the Mayoress was presented with a miniature silver cradle for having given birth during the term of office of her husband, Thomas Berry Horsfall.

We did manage to locate the source of Ann's second nightmare:

Q: 'Where are you?'
A: 'In ... a ... basement.'
Q: 'Where is this room?'
A: 'In a house.'
Q: 'I know it's in a house, but in which town? Where is this house?'
A: 'Oh ... oh ... it ... Chaucer Road.'
Q: 'Chaucer Road. But where? Which town?'
A: 'Don't know.' [She begins to shout.] 'Don't like this room. Don't ... like this room.'
Q: 'Who is with you?'
A: 'Lindy ... and Tony ... and Jimmy ... an' Jacky.'
Q: 'Why are you afraid?'
A: 'Don't like this room!'
Q: 'I know you don't, Sarah, but why are you so frightened? Why don't you like this room?'
A: 'It's that man. It's that man!'
Q: 'What man?'
A: 'Oh ... oh ... oh.' [She begins to cry.] 'Get the kids out.'
Q: 'All right, Sarah, we'll get the kids out.'
A: 'Oh ... he's got ... he's got a big ... it's like a knife.' [She screams.] 'He's hitting me ... He's coming ... He's coming!'

Like all other volunteers who experience past-life regression, Ann Dowling was put through a marathon each time she underwent hypnosis. Questions were thrown at her one after the other; she was switched from one period of Sarah's life to another, and often she was taken to further characters who emerged from the sessions. Throughout such ordeals, Ann never stumbled, never made a mistake and, when telling of the life of Sarah, immediately spoke with the vocabulary, accent and grammar of a nineteenth-century Liverpudlian waif.

One of the characters Ann also regressed to was a rather pompous eighteenth-century slaver-ship captain. The following exchange shows just how accurate Ann could be as regards dates:

Q: 'What year is it?'
A: 'You don't know the year, man? It is the year of Our Lord 1782.'
Q: 'What month is it?'
A: 'What month is it? Where the devil are you from? It is Sunday 16 June.'
Q: 'I suppose you have been to church then?'
A: 'You don't find many churches in the middle of the Caribbean.'

In all the sessions we conducted with Ann Dowling, and of all the characters who emerged from her unconscious, the factual errors she made were insignificant. For a woman who left school at an early age, her knowledge of dates, weather reports and historical events is quite staggering.

The theory of parallel universes is exciting, for it turns our present knowledge of the world upside-down. It might be possible to enter one of those parallel universes, but as yet we cannot be sure; if physicists are exploring its potential, we should certainly keep an open mind.

To explain the astonishing past-life regressions of Ann Dowling, however, we must surely look further, because one question still remains: did Sarah Williams really exist?

Cosmic memory
In the last section we considered a theory which still forms part of the current discussion of nuclear physics. The theory of cosmic memory has an equally scientific base. According to the first law of thermodynamics, 'heat is a form of energy', and energy can be neither manufactured nor destroyed. It can only be changed from one form into another.

Those who believe in cosmic memory take this principle and apply it to the process of thought. The brain produces brainwaves which may be measured on an instrument and which are in essence a form of energy. If energy can be neither manufactured nor destroyed, the brainwaves we produce every day must exist in some form beyond their immediate conception. Every thought, every experience that was ever recorded, continues to exist *somewhere*; perhaps, rather like short-wave radio broadcasts, they are to be found on some 'wavelength' in the ether. But perhaps, too, they find their destination.

Is there a central recording device which stores the memories of time and which passes out its information to those who are receptive to it? Are the cases of past-life regression recorded in this book examples of individuals who have somehow contacted a form of cosmic computer?

A difficult theory to accept of course but, as we should know by now, difficulty is no reason for rejecting an explanation. One fact in its favour is the uncanny chronological accuracy of regressees. Under hypnosis, subjects are asked to go back to specific dates, and every time they go straight to that date, with an accuracy which does seem to suggest the logical functioning of a computer.

We have no specific case studies which either prove or disprove the cosmic memory theory; it could apply to all or none. Pat Roberts' story provides a useful test.

Pat was twenty-six when she first came to one of our regression sessions. She lived with her husband in one of Liverpool's suburbs and knew little about local history. She proved an excellent subject for hypnosis and, when asked to go back to times before she was born, began to recall the life of a girl named Frances. We asked her what her surname was, but she continually avoided giving us an answer:

Q: 'What is your second name, Frances?'
A: 'You keep asking this, don't you? My father is Joe, the cobbler, and he lives in Bankfield Street.'

On another occasion she was more specific:

Q: 'Do you know what your address is? The number on your
    door and the street?'
A: 'Got something to tell people if I get lost.'
Q: 'What is it?'
A: [She begins to sing a rhyme.] 'Frances-Mary-Rodriguez-
    10-Bankfield-Street-Bootle.'

Gore's Liverpool directories for the years 1888 and 1889
show that number 10 Bankfield Street, Bootle, was the home of
a cobbler name Joe Rodriguez.

In later years, when Frances' fortunes had improved
considerably, she was never fully accepted by the middle-class
society in which she then moved. The reason obviously lies
here, in her Portuguese maiden name.

From Pat's sessions we discovered that Frances did not go to
school – by no means uncommon in mid-nineteenth-century
Britain – but that she did gain some education:

Q: 'Have you ever been to school?'
A: 'Mm.'
Q: 'Where?'
A: 'Just to that lady. Don't like her.'
Q: 'What is her name?'
A: 'Mrs Van … Van … something. I don't know.'
Q: 'And where does she live?'
A: 'Don't know. My dad took me.'
Q: 'Did you walk?'
A: 'No. It was a long way. But I couldn't do my letters and I
    told my dad I didn't like it. He said I didn't have to go there
    any more.'

Again, Gore's directories for the 1850s record than an
Elizabeth Van Gelder ran a 'ladies' seminary' at 28 Aigburth
Street, near Smithdown Lane. From Bankfield Street this
would have been about a three-mile walk.

Frances married when she was fairly young, and when asked

about it, she said she was married in 'the little relief church' in Bootle. The staff of Bootle Reference Library hadn't heard of such a place but spent several weeks trying to locate a reference to it. Finally they came across the church of St Mary's erected in 1827 to accommodate the overflow of worshippers from another church of the same name at Walton-on-the-Hill. The 'relief church' was destroyed during the last war, and today there is no trace of St Mary's. The librarian in Bootle assured us that until we had raised this query she had never heard of 'the little relief church' and that in the twenty years she had worked there no one had enquired about it.

One member of our group asked Frances if she had ever been for a ride on an overhead railway:

A: 'The Dingle ... Seaforth ... the Dockers' Umbrella.'
Q: 'That's right. Have you been on it?'
A: 'Yes, I have. It's a bit rickety, isn't it?'
Q: 'Yes.'
A: [She begins to sing.] 'On the Dingle Seaforth Overhead Line, the Overhead Line ... That's a song, you know.'

Now, according to most records, this line (which is now defunct) came into operation only in the 1890s, so how could Frances have ridden on it, as she claimed, in the 1860s? A little research revealed what few still realize, that in 1855 the dock branch of the Yorkshire & Cheshire Railway was opened eighteen feet above the level of the dock quay. So 'the dockers' umbrella', as it was affectionately called, was operational, just as Frances said.

Pat Roberts' past-life regression sessions produced a wealth of remarkable detail, which we went to great lengths to check. She spoke of a 'mission church', which did exist as the Bootle-cum-Lineacre Mission in Ash Street, on the site of the present Baptist church. In the 1850s, the period to which Pat was referring, worshippers used to meet in people's homes and various halls; the venue was always known as 'the mission'. Pat mentioned the names of coffee-houses and stores that have long since disappeared. She mentioned moving from one house in Canning Street to another, and Gore's records confirm a move from 32 to 65 Canning Street. She referred to herself as Frances during some regressions, and Franny in others; the records tally on this difference.

She also spoke of personal feelings, such as her resentment against her middle-class environment after her second marriage, to an accountant named Frederick Jones:

Q: 'Now that you have married into what is effectively a rich
       family, are you moving in different circles?'
A: 'Trying to.'
Q: 'What about big societies or ladies' groups?'
A: 'No, I'm not accepted.'
Q: 'Because of your accent?'
A: 'Mm, and my sallow skin.'
Q: 'Does that anger you?'
A: 'They can take me or leave me, I couldn't give a bugger.'

The mention of her skin, of course, would refer to her Portuguese lineage.

But perhaps most poignant of all is Frances' last appearance. The parish register shows that in the churchyard of St Mary's Bootle there stood a headstone bearing the name 'Frances Jones, died 17th of September 1913.' The headstone, along with the church, was destroyed during World War II, ten years before Pat's birth, so she cannot have seen it, even if she had known of a woman called Frances Jones. But it is the inscription which tells the real tale: 'Gone but not forgotten.'

We have proved, beyond all reasonable doubt, that Frances is not forgotten. She comes back to us through the unconscious memories of Pat Roberts, together with all the actions and accents and language she would have used then. How does Pat have access to those memories? Is it by some form of contact with a cosmic computer? If so, perhaps anyone could reach out and revive the memories of Frances Rodriguez. As yet, however, we have never had any cases of people regressing to the same character.

The cosmic memory theory is a step, a useful pointer along the route of discovery we have undertaken. We cannot rely on it to answer our questions, but it does give us an idea of the enormity of the subject we are tackling.

How many more secrets does this hidden mind of ours conceal?

The collective unconscious

The psychiatrist C.G. Jung based much of his theory of the mind around the idea of the collective unconscious. According to this, the past experience of the human race is incorporated into the brain structure which each person inherits as a baby. This experience is inherited in the form of archetypes, or typical modes of human behaviour. Examples of these are the animus and anima – the 'male' and 'female' influences – the wise old man and the great mother. Many others, he felt, exist within the unconscious, creating a pool of behaviour types which exert influence on the conscious mind.

Each individual, according to Jung, creates his own 'persona' out of his experiences of the world, and presents to other people the character he wishes himself to be. This persona arises from the individual's personal unconscious, but it is also influenced by the archetypes of the collective unconscious which co-exist alongside. The opposite of the persona, which Jung called the 'shadow', consists of all those characteristics of the personal and collective unconscious which the individual wishes to keep hidden from other people.

A well-balanced person, therefore, would not repress too much of his character, creating a shadow self bulging with unreleased traits; he would be confident enough of the persona he presented to the world every day to allow it to show weakness as well as strength.

To put it simply, many different personality types are stored deep within every one of us, all capable of being aroused and brought to the surface. In the mind of every hero is a coward; for every kind person, a sadist; for every wit, a dullard.

The case of Sue Atkins is a perfect example of what could be the collective unconscious and conflicting personality types at work. She is highly intelligent, speaks several languages fluently and is the senior editor of a major English-French dictionary. The characters to whom she regresses – an illiterate orphan boy named Charlie and a stern seventeenth-century Jesuit priest – are almost diametric opposites of the kind of person she is herself.

Charlie lived at the beginning of this century, in a village he calls Willingford. We have been unable to trace such a village, even though he gives detailed descriptions of his surroundings – a river, with caves nearby in which he once hid with a band of gypsies. The village church was called St Michael's. (The village of Wichenford, near Worcester, has the river Severn close by, sandstone caves and a church called St Michael's, so Charlie could be mispronouncing the name.)

Charlie is as unlike Sue as could be. He speaks a rough-and-ready sort of English, swears and shows no signs of any great intelligence. Here he is showing a typically blasphemous approach to the church:

Q: 'What is the name of the church?'
A: 'St Michael's. I know who St Michael was – he was the angel with the sword.'
Q: 'What kind of church is it?'
A: 'Well … it's just a church. It smells inside and it smells outside and it's got bodies all around it.'
Q: 'What religion is it?'
A: 'Just a church. Got bodies all around it; it's planted in the middle of bodies. You got to walk through dead bodies to get in and then they give you pieces of somebody's dead body if you're old enough. And then they say, I am the resurrection and the life. And it seems to me a load of old b …'

Even raucous Charlie couldn't bring himself to be quite blasphemous enough in the end. At another point, Charlie talks about religion:

A: 'You can call people bleedin' bastards, but if you call them bleedin' Jesuses, it comes down … that's what St Michael's for … I once called somebody a bleedin' Jesus, and the teacher took me out and put me 'ead into school bucket … right there … and it were winter, and she put it in three times, and then she said, "spit out that word" and I spat it out, right back into bloody bucket.'

With Father Antony Bennet the subject of religion reoccurs. (If Jung's theory is to be accepted, it must be a particularly difficult theme for Sue Atkins.) Antony is very different from both Sue and Charlie. Born in the first half of the seventeenth century, he had a conventional and restricted upbringing, becoming a Jesuit priest on the wishes of his father. By the time he was middle-aged, however, he had begun to express doubts and fears.

Q: 'What are you doing?'
A: 'I am praying for strength.'
Q: 'Strength for what?'
A: 'Strength to live.'
Q: 'Why is it difficult to live?'
A: 'I have fears. I fear the emptiness.'
Q: 'What are you afraid of?'
A: 'Afraid of God's absence. If God turns His look away from you.'
Q: 'But you have done nothing to make God turn from you.'
A: 'I have doubted.'
Q: 'Don't you think He will understand?'
A: 'I have led a barren life. We must surmount the barren.'
Q: 'How do you mean?'
A: 'My life of prayer is empty.'

Q: 'Why? Have you done no deeds?'
A: 'Deeds are of no account. I have … every priest knows from his confessional … succour to his people … that into one's spiritual life … can become barren … deserts, and a priest is God's help … waters the desert of his people … but there is no one to water my desert. God has turned away.'
Q: 'Why do you think that, Father?'
A: 'I fear God because He is not looking. I fear God because I must live although He is not looking.'
Q: 'But why should God not look at you?'
A: [He is now very upset.] 'God has left me! God has left me!'
Q: 'God has not left you.'
A: [He sobs.] 'God has left me. I fear the Antichrist.'

At a later point, when the priest was seriously ill, he seemed to have come to terms with his predicament:

A: 'I have no fears about the future. God will take me to Him, and that will be the beginning. I know it will be the beginning. I am not afraid. I believe in God. I am tired of this earth, its weariness, the quarrelling and the fighting and the worldliness.'

Or is there the unmistakable tone there of someone trying very hard to convince himself?

Interestingly enough, Sue feels no affinity with the impudent Charlie, and in fact rather dislikes him. But there is one character in her regressions she despises so much she refuses under any circumstances to experience it a second time. The character is a lewd prostitute living in the nineteenth century, whose life, language and habits are all so at odds with Sue's that she found her one encounter too upsetting to repeat.

The experiences of Sue Atkins under hypnosis seemed to

show that her unconscious mind had an opposite for everything in which she believed. Her own personal philosophy, her vocation, her spiritual beliefs, even her language – all these were mocked by the characters she carried within her. Perhaps the struggle between Sue's persona – her everyday character – and her shadow self is at the root of these regressions; again, we cannot be sure. Perhaps, as has been suggested elsewhere, the characters of Charlie and Antony are *inherited* personalities, passed on through her genes just as her physical make-up was passed on? Scientists have no evidence that the DNA structure of cells can accommodate this kind of information, but they are not one hundred per cent certain. If it were possible for psychological traits to be inherited alongside physiological features, could the characters of Charlie and Antony be passive elements co-existing alongside the dominating inherited character which is Sue's? Just as red hair in one person may be a recessive strain, unlikely to produce red hair in any offspring, a personality could be recessive, only reappearing some generations on.

We are, of course, dealing in speculation now, and going against the grain of current scientific thinking. In our search for understanding, however, nothing can be excluded from consideration, and we will deal with this theory of genetic inheritance a little later on.

But to illustrate the main Jungian thesis of this section, we will go over some of the more interesting cases relating to conflicting personality types. Cases of this kind, where the character who emerges from regression seems to differ so completely from the person under hypnosis, are a tiny minority of the regressions I have recorded; they should not be taken as typical.

Dianne is an intelligent, well-educated and polite young woman who has a responsible job in a law firm. She teaches in her local Sunday School. Under hypnosis she regresses to someone called Ella:

Q: 'Ella, are you married?'

A: 'No, I've got enough wi' this bloody lot.'
Q: 'Which bloody lot?'
A: 'Those bloody kids. Me mother's buggered off.'
Q: 'Where's your father?'
A: 'He's bloody drunk ag'in.'

Ella, it seems, lived on a barge, on the Grand Union Canal and was only ever known as 'Ella the Boat'. She could neither read nor write and appeared to have absolutely no knowledge of the world at large. She was coarse, vulgar and uneducated, the antithesis of Dianne.

On one occasion we found her lying in a strange bed with a king-sized hangover. She had no idea where she was or whom she had slept with. All she could remember was drinking the previous night at a canal-side inn, celebrating the wedding of one Margaret Bower.

A similar case occurred with George. Throughout his adult life he had been shy and unable to mix with women. Under hypnosis, he regressed to someone called Martin and in doing so switched quite naturally to a gruff and uncouth style of delivery. Martin said he was eighteen years old and apprenticed to a blacksmith in a Cheshire village. He had many girlfriends, and one in particular called Kathy, who was attractive, with long blonde hair. When we sent him to any time he was in Kathy's company, he found himself on the banks of a stream which he called Grinley Brook. As we listened to his half of his conversation with Kathy, we were struck by the confidence which contrasted so strongly with George's own shyness. Throughout the memories of Martin, right up to his death in a fire at the forge where he ran his own business, the same strong character showed itself time and again. Though he married Kathy, he went philandering at every opportunity he could find.

Wishful thinking? Undoubtedly the discovery of Martin has helped George overcome his crippling shyness towards women; by adding just a hint of that arrogant personality to his own, he has changed his outlook on the world. But observers of his regression are all reluctant to ascribe it to wish-fulfilment. The ease with which George slips into the memories of Martin, the authentic descriptions of his surroundings, the honest responses under quick-fire questioning – these are all involuntary.

Mike is a hard-working American executive, a no-nonsense man who drinks little and maintains a firm control over his life. At his first regression session he immediately took on the character of Stephen, a Dublin down-and-out and drunkard. No actor could have portrayed Stephen more realistically, as he stumbled from drink to drink, cadging money and eating in soup kitchens. Full of wit and charm when he wanted, Stephen's was a sad tale, ending in severe alcoholic illness and poverty. During the lengthy sessions we conducted with Mike, all kinds of fascinating detail about Dublin life emerged – much of it later verified against the records, and the picture we finally assembled was one of the most thorough we have. But what was most remarkable was the contrast between sober, hard-working Mike and drunk, scrounging Stephen. A coincidence?

Philip is another successful businessman. Intelligent and well educated, he has a horror of drugs of any kind, but under hypnosis he regressed to Silas, an East Anglian tramp who spent his summers wandering about the countryside eating hallucinogenic mushrooms! According to Silas, the mushrooms gave him a feeling of euphoria, and he would sit for hours 'watching the flowers grow'. A character like Silas would not appear in the records, so we have had no luck in tracing him, but he is able to provide very accurate descriptions of districts Philip has never visited. We came across a book of nineteenth-century place-names in East Anglia which showed that many of them were different from their modern counterparts; when we put some of the old names to Silas, he responded as he had not done to suggestions of twentieth-century names. Again, an interesting regression in itself, but with the added curiosity of the personality distinctions.

Andrew Selby, a civil engineer for the water board in London, is a perfectionist in everything he does: home repairs, decorations, rewiring, plumbing, painting – everything he turns his hand to, he has to do painstakingly well. There is nothing he will not tackle, nothing defeats him. But one aspect of his character puzzled him: he felt uneasy in the company of disabled people and could not understand why he should feel so uncomfortable about physical disability.

Under hypnosis he regressed to Geoffrey, a helpless victim of what would appear to have been cerebral palsy. He was confined to a wheelchair, had difficulty in speaking and showed all the uncontrollable body movements characteristic of spasticity. After the regression, Andrew found he had lost his fear of disability, perhaps because he can claim to have experienced it himself. And he retained his other abilities too: if anything, the experience has heightened his determination to let no task beat him.

Our last example is John Kingsale, the premier baron of Ireland, who regressed very easily when he attended one of my sessions. Because of his class, we expected him to regress to a character we could easily research from his family tree. Instead, he brought out the memories of a farm labourer called Tom Jenkins, who supplemented his meagre income with a spot of smuggling. When we first came upon him, it was night-time and he, with the rest of the gang, was waiting at a small cove in Sussex. No one present, including Lord Kingsale, had ever heard of the cove, but a quick check in a gazetteer showed that it did indeed exist. The gang was waiting for a boatload of contraband from France but was surprised by a cutter full of revenue men, all armed with pistols. Tom was shot in the chest and killed.

The theory of the collective unconscious is a fascinating one, and of great importance in understanding the modern psyche. It must have some bearing on the cases we have discussed here, and it probably answers some of the questions which hypnotic regression arouses. But it cannot help us when we come to this point: many of the cases mentioned so far have revealed information which the subject could not have previously known.

The influence of unconscious archetypes cannot extend to producing accurate historical data, so, necessarily, the regressions must be based on a different source.

It is that source we are still trying to find.

Spiritualism

The belief in the spirit world is not as widespread as once it was. In the 1920s and 1930s it was very fashionable to attend a séance now and again, and if people did not commit themselves utterly to the belief, they did at least pay it a good deal of respect. Even now, there are several mediums who appear regularly in our newspapers, and many more who make a good living from apparently putting people in touch with the dead. But perhaps we live in a more cynical age, for the salad days of spiritualism seem to have passed.

Like the theory of reincarnation, spiritualism states that there is a continued existence of some human element after death. But spiritualists insist that the life force – or whatever it is that survives the death of the body – inhabits another kind of universe and can communicate with us only through intermediaries, or mediums.

These mediums do seem to see the people who, as they say, are on 'the other side'. The question is: are they seeing them in the same extraordinary way as my regression subjects 'see' individuals from the past? The following example might illuminate us.

During the period when I lectured on extra-sensory perception for Liverpool Education Authority in a series of adult education classes, I regularly invited clairvoyants to demonstrate their abilities to my students. There was no question of trickery or foreknowledge in any of them. They were not stage performers, just genuine individuals who were quite sincere in their beliefs.

On one particular occasion I invited a friend of mine who was highly regarded within spiritualist circles. In the audience was a mother and a daughter. They did not resemble each other physically and seldom sat together in the classroom; in fact, not many people knew they were related. The spiritualist began to tell the mother about her late husband and came out with such an accurate portrait of the man that she was quite shocked by what she heard. He described a healthy, vigorous man, just as the woman remembered. Later on, the spiritualist addressed the daughter, not knowing of the family relationship. He described her father as she last knew him, which was when he was sick, with an amputated leg. Again, the portrait was accurate. When the daughter was very young, her mother and father had divorced, and she had been brought up by her mother alone. Many years later, the daughter searched out her father and found him disabled, with only one leg. Her mother never saw the man in that state and had memories of him only as a fit young man.

If the spiritualist had been communicating with the dead man, he would have known that the women were related. What seems to have been happening, then, was that he picked up on their conscious or unconscious memories and produced portraits of what he thought were two separate individuals.

The ability to key into other people's thoughts is interesting in itself, and we will talk about telepathy in the next section, but 'seeing' a person in the way that spiritualist 'saw' the dead man is very different from hypnotic regression. People come away from my sessions having experienced the life of another person, having seen what that person saw, smelt the same smells, felt the same emotions.

Spiritualists do not, of course, accept the telepathy explanation. They insist that a subject under regressive hypnosis becomes a hyper-sensitive medium, able to bypass the normal spirit guide and be taken over by a free-roaming spirit. Like several of the other theories we have been considering, spiritualism could apply to every case of regression. But it has one main weakness as far as we are concerned. If a wandering spirit takes over the unconscious mind during hypnotic regression, it must get trapped there, because all successful regressees have been able to go back to such memories once they have been discovered. Not only that: their sense of chronology and the accuracy of those memories remain unimpaired no matter how long the gap between regressions. Now, since most people seem able to regress to several different lives, they must have several wandering spirits trapped in their unconscious minds. You don't have to be a mathematician to realize that the population of the spirit world would be lowered pretty quickly at this rate.

The impulse to put one's faith in spiritualism is understandable. Remember, we are dealing with an incredible phenomenon: ordinary people, like you or me, are reliving the past lives of people who are dead. They are going through experiences which often change their lives and certainly change the way they think. Their everyday world view is not sophisticated enough to cope with such events, and they often struggle to make any sense of it at all. But one of my intentions with this book is to show that, no matter how extraordinary it is, hypnotic regression can be assessed without leaping to hasty conclusions.

The case for spiritualism, it seems to me, is too thin. It may have an appealing glamour, but it doesn't seem to get at the heart of these cases of hypnotic regression. There is still something missing, some intangible element that causes the past to be brought back to life. So that when the words 'You are going back ...' sound the start of another session, the person in the chair once again enters a world which only he can know. If we can probe the mystery, we might make it a world which we all can share.

Telepathy
Telepathy is a catch-all word which describes a variety of interesting functions of the mind. Think of the times when the name of an old friend enters your head for no reason, and then within a few days you hear from him for the first time in years. And what about those times when you decide on an action at

exactly the same time as someone else undertakes it. Or when two people start speaking at the same time and find they are saying the same thing. Like the experience of *déjà vu*, these telepathic moments are unsettling.

A recent experiment with dolphins seems to suggest that they have a more advanced telepathic ability. Two dolphins were placed in tanks of water separated by material which would not allow sound waves or any other kind of vibrations to pass from one to the other. In the tanks was a series of buttons which operated coloured lights. When one dolphin lit any light, the other consistently activated the same one.

It is likely that a certain amount of this kind of telepathic activity goes on at my hypnotic regression sessions, partly because each one lasts several hours and consists of a small group of people sitting together in one room. But is telepathy sufficient to produce some of the dazzling tales we have witnessed so far? And if it is, why do the regressions so often consist of quite banal information, often crudely presented and not always completely accurate? Specialists are frequently to be found at my sessions – writers, historians, scientists – but their knowledge very rarely enters the answers of subjects under regression.

At a session in America, attended by several teachers of English literature, a woman under regression said she was reading a book of poems by one particular author. The teachers in the group all denied that this author had published any work by the year in which the woman found herself. They concluded, therefore, that the regression was a fantasy. When the woman came out of her regression, she agreed with the opinion of her colleagues. But later, when we checked in the *Encyclopaedia Britannica*, we found they were all wrong: the author *had* published a volume of poetry by the date stated during the regression.

Obviously, subjects are able to produce accurate information under hypnosis without having to rely on telepathy. But in order to satisfy our sternest critics, we make every effort to extract details during a regression before undertaking research; this way, we cannot be accused of passing information from one mind to another.

One case where telepathy did occur was itself illuminating. Peter Moss, the historian who has written a book featuring a selection of my regressions, was present when Ann Dowling was being taken back to the life of the street urchin Sarah Williams. Peter was called out of the room by the telephone, and during his absence Sarah mentioned someone in Everton called Doubleday. When Peter came back, he said the phone call had been from an editor at Doubleday, the American publishers.

On the other hand, there have been hundreds of occasions when everyone in the room has been willing a subject to give the right answers, always to no avail. The person who stated under hypnosis that Queen Victoria was alive in 1914 could not be shifted from her opinion, even though everyone in the room knew she was wrong. I brought her out of hypnosis to discuss her mistake, and she couldn't understand how it had come about. But then, once she was put back to that character, she repeated the mistake.

We shouldn't ignore telepathy. We may find in the future that our capacity for it is considerably greater than we imagined, and that it can be put to good use. For the present, it is a phenomenon that needs careful research.

But while it can be proved to be operating in certain circumstances, it is by no means the key we are seeking. Just as the Rosetta stone opened up the world of Egyptian hieroglyphs, there is an answer somewhere to the riddle of hypnotic regression. When we reach it, I'm sure we'll be dazzled by its simplicity. For the present, we're blinded by the light of our extraordinary experience.

Genetically inherited memory
Inheritance is an idea deeply rooted in our culture. We expect to inherit the worldly goods of our parents – anything from a country mansion to a set of dinner plates, and we preserve the

memory of other relations by the trinkets which are passed down for our safe-keeping. But we are already accustomed to the idea from birth, for we soon know that our physical appearance is directly inherited from our parents, who are themselves carrying genetic instructions from their parents and their grandparents, and so on.

'He's got his mother's eyes', 'the image of his father', 'hair just like his grandad' – we've all heard these comments and remarked on the likenesses existing within families, but how often do we consider the mechanism which brings about this astonishing replication? The genes of your father and your mother, combining within that first cell in your mother's womb, contain all the information needed to predict exactly how you will look. What kind of computer software can we produce to match the sophistication of the genetic process?

But it's not just our looks which are passed on. Family traits are identified in people, particularly as they grow older, and the legendary stubbornness of a grandmother, or the mechanical skill of a father, or the meanness of a great-grandfather, is supposedly revived in a later generation. Our knowledge of this region of genetics is still uncertain, but some family characteristics are too sharply defined to be mere coincidence. What, then, of the possibility that, alongside physical and psychological traits, memory itself can be inherited?

The animal kingdom provides a useful starting point for this discussion. How do birds know how to build nests? What makes young starlings fly south in the autumn and return the following spring? Who tells salmon to return to their place of birth to spawn? Ornithologists have no evidence of birds instructing each other in the art of nest-building, and yet each generation of birds is capable of finding a good site for a nest, locating the appropriate building materials, cementing the structure firmly together. We humans would need a course of detailed evening classes to attempt such a feat of civil engineering!

Somehow, then, the bird 'picks up' the information it needs. It could be by telepathy, as in the case of the dolphins we discussed earlier, but it seems unlikely that the animal kingdom is talking to itself so systematically without our noticing it. No, somehow, each bird is born with the inherited knowledge of how to build a nest, knowing too that when the weather begins to turn cold there are warmer climes for it to inhabit. But is this knowledge intrinsic to the genetic make-up of birds as a species – that is, is it an instruction which is replicated in every bird – or is it a specific memory passed on from one bird to another? If so, then each bird would build its nest in the fashion of its mother and father, just as its mother and father learned the skill from their parents.

Again, the present scientific view is that there is no capability within the DNA structure of cells which can incorporate the memory of the individual. DNA is a chain of molecules which acts as the source of genetic instructions; it cannot, say the scientists, continue to evolve according to the experiences of the individual. We are left, once more, with a familiar imponderable: if something *can't* happen, why is it that so often it appears that it does?

During the course of my sessions of hypnotic regression, I have come across several cases which could be said to support the theory of genetically inherited memory. One such is that of Liz Howard.

Ironically, Liz is a human biologist by profession. The events of her regressions caused her considerable confusion, for they seemed to run counter to everything she had ever known about biology and genetics. The most important fact, however, was her maiden name: Fitton.

Under hypnosis, Liz regressed to a character called Elizabeth Fytton, whose family lived at Gawsworth Hall in Cheshire. She said she was a handmaiden to Anne Boleyn in the sixteenth century, and proceeded to give us a very graphic and detailed description of life at the Court of Henry VIII. For example, we asked her about the Queen's hands, knowing that legend has it that she had six fingers on one hand. Elizabeth Fytton denied this but, when pressed on the subject, said: 'Oh that. Everybody says she has too many fingers in too many pies.' Thus are legends created, perhaps?

We questioned Elizabeth very thoroughly, using a dictionary of historical slang to test the authenticity of the regression. For example, we asked her about a 'gander-mooner', and she replied, correctly if less than politely, that it referred to the accepted custom of the day for the husband to be unfaithful to his wife during the month after childbirth. On a hundred other such questions, she responded correctly to words and phrases now long gone from our vocabulary.

The present owners of Gawsworth Hall are Tim and Elizabeth Richards. Fascinated by the stories of Liz Howard's regression, they attended sessions and contributed to our research. Liz herself had never visited the Hall, a sixteenth-century manor now open to the public, but still managed to give an accurate description of how it would have looked 400 years ago. Tim and Elizabeth confirmed her descriptions from their family records.

For example, Liz insisted that the Hall was black and yellow, rather than black and white as one would expect. A few weeks before that particular regression, the Richards had discovered that yellow had been the second colour of the Hall during the sixteenth century, changing to white only at a later date.

After giving a detailed description of the local church, Liz visited it, only to find it 'the wrong way round'. The Richards pointed out a bricked-up doorway at the opposite end of the church, which the Fyttons would have used. Liz also insisted that the beams were a different colour, which confused her until she was shown a piece of the original beam coloured as she had said.

As Elizabeth Fytton, Liz correctly named various members of the Fytton family and gave numerous details of events which the Richards had confirmed from their own records.

This remarkable series of regressions encouraged Liz to put her experiences into writing, and she has since achieved success with historical novels such as *Elizabeth Fytton of Gawsworth Hall*.

She could, in fact, be said to be the only historical novelist writing from memory! Here is her written testimony to me of her regressions:

How time flies! Can it really be more than four years since I came to you with the strange tale of a dream which came true? And how could any of us possibly have foretold where my insatiable curiosity would lead? Those hypnotic regressions, created in a unique atmosphere where your skill blended with my open mind, have become an integral part of my life. There is still no concrete explanation for what happened on that couch over a period of more than two years. I insisted that my name was Elizabeth Fytton and that I lived at Gawsworth Hall, during Tudor times! Giving descriptions of Cheshire buildings in the sixteenth century, and life at the Courts of Henry VIII and Queen Elizabeth I. Wasn't it all too ridiculous? If you remember, I refused to believe a word of my hypnotic ramblings, regarding the pictures in my head, no matter how realistic, as pure fantasy. Despite the emphatic detail of people and places catalogued by 'Elizabeth Fytton', who would have thought that hours of painstaking research would only prove my unconscious mind right? How such a wealth of information could have been absorbed and stored while the conscious mind remained completely ignorant of the fact will always be a mystery. Or is there really another explanation, as so many wish to believe? Reincarnation, or inherited memory?

As the idea of reincarnation is beyond the bounds of my own beliefs, and as there are no scientific means available for examining such a theory, I concentrated on the possibility of inherited memory. After much delving into the biochemistry of the central nervous system, I have reluctantly come to the conclusion that, though the subject is still on the far horizons of man's understanding, there is a possibility that an excessive and unaccountable amount of RNA in ova could be the vehicle for memory transfer. Should this be the case, any such inheritance would obviously pass solely through the female line; an interesting thought when considering my own experiences. However, this is still only theory, and for the time being we can only continue to wonder.

Liz is right, of course: there can be no certainty in the mysterious world of hypnotic regression. But one strong objection to the theory of genetically inherited memory is that, logically, it should be impossible for subjects to recall death under hypnosis. For if they are calling on memories which they have inherited, then those memories can go only as far as the date of giving birth; they certainly cannot incorporate a death. But as we have already seen, people do relive deaths under hypnosis, just as Dianne, in the following case, has.

Dianne is a young married woman from North Wales. As a child she would regularly disappear from her home and was invariably found by her family sitting at the grave of an aunt called Jacqueline, who had died at the age of five, well before Dianne was born.

Under hypnosis, Dianne regressed to someone called Jacqueline who, it soon transpired, was the same aunt who had died as a child. Dianne produced a highly detailed account of Jacqueline's five years of life, an account which was verified throughout from family records. When we brought her to the time of her death, she produced all the symptoms of TB meningitis, symptoms which were confirmed by a doctor in our midst. But most poignantly of all, when the moment of death arrived, Jacqueline was heard to murmur: 'Cora, don't cry.'

Cora is Dianne's mother, Jacqueline's sister. She and other members of the family had always borne a grudge against the doctor who failed to diagnose Jacqueline's illness and who was probably responsible for allowing it to develop so quickly. When asked about the moment of Jacqueline's death, Cora said her sister had been silent and that the only words spoken were by other members of the family, cursing the doctor. I put Cora under hypnosis, and she regressed without difficulty to that moment in her own childhood when her sister was dying. True enough, she began to curse the doctor who had accused Jacqueline of malingering. But then, she told us what she could hear her sister saying: 'Cora, don't cry.'

Was Dianne merely recalling family woes which must have been discussed countless times in her youth? If so, how could she be so accurate about her aunt's life, and how could she reveal Jacqueline's dying words, when even her mother had forgotten them? Or is it possible that poor Jacqueline's memories have somehow been inherited by her niece, to be recalled from her unconscious mind with the encouragement of hypnosis?

I have known one other case similar to Dianne's. A young woman attended one of my sessions and told us that, ever since she was a little girl, she had refused to call her mother anything but 'sister'. Under regression, she became an aunt who had died before she was born. At this session the facts she came out with were impressive and accurate but could always be said to have been picked up from hearing family conversations about her late aunt. What was so fascinating was the fact that, even as a child, she had thought of her own mother as a sister.

If it *is* possible for memories to be passed on, we should be able to find examples of individuals using the information they have inherited. The cases of child prodigies such as Mozart would seem to point this way: he was writing music by the age of 3½, and both his father and grandfather were accomplished musicians. I myself have come across few such cases, but the following are certainly of interest.

A young woman from Chester regressed to a character who said she had just left a finishing school in Brighton and that her favourite subject was sketching. She was told to keep this ability when she came out of her regression and, to her amazement, the young woman drew a beautiful sketch of a garden once she had been aroused from hypnosis. Yet for as long as she can remember, she has had difficulty even in drawing a straight line! A couple of years later I asked her whether her artistic talents remained, and she said that they had flourished for some months after the sessions, but she had then stopped sketching.

All subsequent attempts to revive the ability failed: the gift had deserted her.

Mary Starling, who knew nothing of music, regressed to a little blind girl who could play the piano. She too was told to retain the ability. The next time after the session when she found a piano, she sat down to play but could produce nothing, despite the strong feeling that she was capable of it. Mary became frustrated and understandably screwed her eyes tightly shut in concentration. As soon as her eyes were closed, she found herself playing a few simple tunes, quite spontaneously.

Finally, there was the young woman from Stockport who, although left-handed all her life, regressed to a right-handed character. When aroused from hypnosis, she found to her delight that she had become ambidextrous.

The theory of genetic inheritance can explain many things, but it cannot answer that one objection of the impossibility of inheriting the experience of death. Of course, given the fantastic numbers of people who could theoretically be said to be one's ancestors – remember our discussion of history and family trees earlier in the book – there might be some cause for suggesting that memory could be inherited racially, rather than just from one's parents or grandparents. Even five or six generations back, the number of one's ancestors was huge, and thus the capacity for memories which, together, could incorporate a whole race would be great.

We will leave this theory with the extraordinary case of the twins whom I regressed for a BBC TV programme on regression. The researchers for the programme had received two very similar letters from identical twins, each suggesting she should try regression. The twins were in their twenties, married and both teachers.

Each woman was regressed out of the presence of the other, and their memories of their own lives proved identical. Then they were taken, again individually, to pre-birth memories, and both regressed to the same characters. The differences in their regressions were absolutely minor: for example, one twin said she was living in the first house of a street in a Welsh village, the other said she was living in the last house of the same street. In the end, we regressed them together, in their own homes. For over an hour, they answered questions under hypnotic regression in turn, always remaining consistent and always, as far as we can tell, accurate. Afterwards, the twins said they had resented the fact that another person was answering the questions for them.

It was an eerie moment, hearing those two women speaking as one. After many years of research into the subject I remain gripped by the phenomenon of regression, and the sight of a regression duplicated before my very eyes was astonishing. It was a graphic illustration of the power of the argument for genetically inherited memory, an argument which we are still unqualified either to accept or to dismiss. But still, the objections of death linger, the limits of the theory remain unsatisfying, and I find myself looking beyond for further knowledge.

It is there somewhere. We have found the dead, we have brought their memories back to life: soon, surely quite soon, we will understand how it happens.

Cryptamnesia

Earlier in the book I talked about the 'hidden mind'. In fact, everything we've been discussing so far relates to abilities that still remain hidden from us, but with this phrase I was describing the mind's incredible capacity for information. The example I used in that earlier chapter was of a tape-recorder at a party, which records an indecipherable mêlée of voices, compared with the conscious mind, which filters out all unnecessary conversation. The unconscious mind is that tape-recorder: it listens, it records and it stores information.

If we were incapable of weeding out the essential from the non-essential, if we had to be consciously aware of *everything* around us, we would be drowned in experience, too busy responding to external stimuli to take the most trivial decision. But also, if we were incapable of remembering information, we would never learn from experience. That's why we rely on the conscious mind to be aware of what is important, and on the unconscious mind to record indiscriminately every experience that comes its way. This mental function is known as cryptamnesia.

In the modern world, every individual is bombarded with information every day, from the moment of waking to the return of sleep. Books, newspapers, radio, television, conversations, work – all these sources of data demand our attention, but only selected ones are retained by our conscious memories. What books did you read last year? What clothes did you buy? How many magazines and newspapers did you get through? This kind of information no longer needs to be retained by your conscious memory, and instead it is stored, logged, in the memory-banks of the unconscious.

Consider the number of times a minor detail from the past 'comes to mind' unexpectedly. Or how a previous experience can be recalled long after it has been forgotten. The information is there; what is in question is our ability to retrieve it.

Many people believe that the cases of hypnotic regression which emerge from my sessions are all examples of cryptamnesia. They state, as an *a priori* condition of their argument, that the memories of a dead person cannot reappear in someone else's unconscious at a later date; therefore the answer must be cryptamnesia.

I do not like this kind of *a priori* argument. But before I tackle its relevance to our discussion, I'd like to show how cryptamnesia can and does manifest itself in hypnotic regression.

A Birmingham nurse came to one of my sessions with a real desire to regress. Her family were convinced she was the reincarnation of an aunt who had died a year before her own birth. They believed this because the nurse had such astonishingly accurate memories of the accident at a picnic which had precipitated her aunt's death.

Under hypnosis, the nurse did take on the character of her aunt. She produced some extraordinary details of that fateful picnic, all of which were verified: she named the place, described the colour of the rug, the make of the car, the identities of the people present, the times of departures and arrivals. The performance was realistic and impressively accurate. But when we took the nurse back to other times in the life of her aunt, again under hypnosis, her replies became muddled. She named the correct relations, marriages and important occasions of the rest of her parents' family but consistently gave the wrong answers about their occupations, and several other subjects. Her dates were hopelessly wrong, both of her family and of world events.

It was then that I regressed her to the first time she had ever heard about the picnic. She was five years old, sitting under the dining-room table at home, pretending to be in a tent. No one knew she was there, as a large tablecloth was hiding her from her mother and another aunt in the same room. The two women were discussing the picnic and accident in great detail, and the little girl, keeping as quiet as a mouse, was listening to every word.

Hearing about the accident at such a young age must have been a shock to the girl, causing her to return to it at a later date in her life. But until she did, the exact memory of that overheard conversation remained in her unconscious mind, down to the very last detail. And when she finally brought it out again during one of my sessions, she was as convincing in her portrayal as could be.

So, yes, cryptamnesia is an answer to some of the regressions I have witnessed. But naturally we lay as many traps as possible in order to identify them, such as sending the subject back to the first time they ever heard of a particular character. And it is usually not difficult to recognize an example of cryptamnesia, particularly since films and novels so often form the staple diet of such regressions. The following case is quite typical.

Judy had difficulty in regressing and was held up for a long time by psychological blocks within her, resisting the course of hypnosis. Finally she solved them and began to regress to what seemed to be a pre-birth memory.

She said her name was Susanna Peterson and that she lived in Rochester, Kent, with her mother and father. The period was around the 1860s, and she thought her father was an academic or a writer. She was a happy, if lonely, young girl who enjoyed embroidery and other quiet hobbies.

As we questioned her more, we discovered that the family's real name was Petrovitch and that they were Russian refugees pretending to be British. At some point, Susanna was sent to Gillingham to live with her aunt and uncle, perhaps because, as we found out later, her mother was mad. When she returned to her home, she found it in flames and discovered that her mother had perished in the fire.

Later we found Susanna in a hospital run by nuns. It was difficult to tell whether she was a patient or a nun, although she did have something wrong with her left leg. She was very lonely at this stage and felt that she was being singled out for punishment by everyone else in the hospital.

A Russian family pretending to be British, a mad mother burned to death, a lonely child mistreated in a convent … the very fact that it was so traumatic made us suspicious of this regression, and soon we began to unravel the clues. Charlotte Brontë's *Jane Eyre* provided the first answer – not only does it have a mad woman dying in a fire, it even has the name of Rochester. Then Judy started to tell us of her own fantasies and how they corresponded with details of the regression; she recalled, too, how lonely she had been as a child and as an adolescent. And the Russian element? Her father, it transpired, is fascinated by the country and has even learned the language. Finally, not one detail of Judy's regression has been historically verified.

As with the cases of fantasy and imagination which we discussed earlier in this chapter, there was certainly no attempt by Judy to mislead us or to be dishonest. But instead of just making the details of her regression up, she was innocently recalling events from her own life and from a book, and merging them into a fantasy which even had herself convinced. Unwittingly, her unconscious mind revealed information which her conscious mind was unable to decipher.

As the next case shows, we always have to be on our guard against the extraordinary influence of cryptamnesia.

A woman regressed to a character called Amelia, living in the same district as she did. Understandably, she was very accurate when answering questions on local details but she fell down when it came to dates. For example, she said she was married in a church which did exist, but at a time before it had even been built. Amelia was a small, fiery woman, married to a merchant sea-captain. At one point she recalled attacking a carter who was beating his unfortunate horse, because the animal was unable to pull a heavy load.

I sent the woman back through the memories of her own life, to the first time she had ever heard about this character, read about her or seen her in a film. It was obvious that she had never before come across Amelia.

Many years later, watching the film *The Lady Killers*, I recognized the merchant sea-captain's wife. Everything brought out in the regression was there, including the incident with the carter and his horse – except the character was not called Amelia. The woman had obviously adopted the story but had changed the name. If we had asked her to go back to the first time she had heard of this incident, she would undoubtedly have recalled seeing it in the film. However, as we only asked her to think of the name Amelia, her unconscious mind failed to make the connection.

From the years I have spent with hypnotic regression, I have witnessed countless cases of cryptamnesia, many of which took some time to recognize. All of them, however, were fascinating examples of how the mind can store information for years, only to bring it out again with complete accuracy. Such cases are entertaining and show us how much we still have to learn about the capacities of our minds.

But the fact that so many of these cases occur does not mean, as some people would argue, that *all* hypnotic regression is cryptamnesia. If it were, then at some point in his life, now utterly forgotten to him, Ray Bryant must have absorbed huge amounts of detail about the Crimean War; Liz Howard must have picked up stories about the Fyttons of Gawsworth Hall; Pat Roberts must, unbeknown to herself, have studied the local history of Liverpool; Ann Dowling must similarly have done a history course, and then forgotten it. For the cryptamnesia explanation to apply to all our cases, the impossible must have occurred.

But perhaps, when faced with the unknown, it is preferable to believe in the impossible rather than to face a more unsettling truth. As I suggested above, those who ascribe all the phenomena of my research to cryptamnesia tend to rule out any possibility of an alternative explanation *from the very start*. I am unwilling to be so certain. Common sense alone shows that there has to be another reason for many of the regressions we are considering: they are simply too specific for us not to be able to recognize if an unconscious memory was at work.

For, above all, these cases are real. You cannot listen to someone over a period of a hundred hours or more, talking of another life in another age, and still hold the view that he is recalling the page of a long-forgotten history book or remembering the details of an historical drama. It just isn't possible. And if I refuse to believe in the impossible, surely I must believe in something? Surely we are ready, at last, to comprehend?

4 Reincarnation

It seems we are left with a difficult choice. Of the theories discussed in the previous chapter, not one can be confidently said to answer all the queries and objections raised by every case of hypnotic regression. Each theory seems to be relevant to some, but none appears to apply to all. At the same time, there are those examples – admittedly a tiny proportion of the numbers I have witnessed over the years – which simply cannot be explained by any logic available to us. The choice, then, is this: do we content ourselves with a half-answer, a half-knowledge, merely because it is more comforting than ignorance, or do we remain inquisitive, carry on with the task, until the weight of experience brings the reward of understanding?

To me, there is no choice. In this chapter we will look at some of the cases which make me determined to continue – cases which, like some of those we have looked at already, defy our present methods of understanding ourselves and the world. They are, I should repeat, a small percentage of the sessions conducted, but they are by far the most important. Until I have the means with which to explain them, I can only think of them in the way they appear before my eyes: as a form of reincarnation.

Over two-thirds of the earth's population believe in reincarnation. It is a belief made comprehensible by nature herself, in the coming and going of the seasons: the stripping bare of trees in the autumn, the return of life in the spring. Myths created around the idea exist all over the world, while the basis of Christianity is the belief in the everlasting soul. It is also a means of coming to terms with death – the idea that our soul can outlive our body makes the brutal fact of death less painful.

Around the world, reincarnation takes on different shades of meaning. In some religions, there is a strong sense of the progression of the soul from one level to another. If we do not learn the lessons of one level, we must go through them again and again until we do; only then does the soul move on to a higher being. There can be a sense of punishment too – a man may become a snake in his next life if he shows himself unworthy of human status.

But other religions interpret reincarnation as a random operation. They state that there is a finite number of souls on the planet which inhabit different bodies from generation to generation. This deals with the problem of progression, and of the superiority of one kind of soul over another, and leaves the fate of this fundamental spirit element to chance.

If the 'soul' exists, and if it does survive the death of the body, then according to these theories of reincarnation it should just as likely be found in the body of an animal as in the body of a man. From time to time, we do come across cases where the subject seems to be regressing to an animal – they are, of course, impossible to test – and when they do occur, they create a strange and mysterious atmosphere.

A man who has regressed to pre-birth memories seemed to be reacting but failed to respond to any of our questions. When he was brought out of hypnosis, he told us that he had found himself standing in a field, watching a farmer approach him. To his left was a stream, and spanning it a bridge, upon which an artist sat painting at an easel. The subject recalled that his eyes were at about the same level as the farmer's, which could suggest that he was a large animal. When my voice entered his head, he recognized the sound as being human – so he must have been used to humans – but he was unable to make sense of it or respond to it. A horse, or a cow?

A businessman, when regressed, found himself lying on a hillside, overlooking trees which later he was unable to recognize. Suddenly the top of a nearby hill blew off, and he felt something hit him in the middle of his back. Then he began to roll down the hill, writhing and hissing as he went. He caught sight of a long tail, which he felt was his own, whipping around in front of him: it was covered in scales.

A woman found herself standing more or less upright, looking inside a dead tree for grubs to eat. She had hair on her face and knew that she was a man. Again, she was unable to communicate with us. Similarly, another woman found herself in a cave, wearing only an animal skin and eating a piece of raw meat from a dead animal. She did not know what the animal was, and when our voices appeared in her head, she became frightened and confused. Once she was aroused from hypnosis, she still had the taste of the dead animal's blood in her mouth.

Another way of considering reincarnation is to think of a tape-recorder. The best machines, when they erase a recording and lay down a new one, erase to a depth of about 85 decibels, which is well below the depth where they are able to interfere with new recordings. But if the tape head has not been cleaned, the depth is lessened, and some of the old recording can be heard coming through on the new. It might even be possible to retrieve every recording ever made on a tape, if we had sufficiently sensitive equipment with which to pick it up. Perhaps hypnosis acts as a highly sensitive medium through which we can pick up the lives, or the souls, lying beneath our own?

I am not about to commit myself to the theory of reincarnation. The following cases are certainly extraordinary – even more so than those we have already considered – and they still make fascinating reading. Some contradict the history books and are subsequently proved to be right; some produce information which can be verified only after months of detailed research. With all of them, we have to remain sceptical until the odds on any one person having access to that information are so high as to be untenable. And when a person of limited education produces historical data known only to historians of a specialist field, and produces it consistently over hours and hours of exhausting questioning, only then do we accept the regression as 'genuine'.

But even though I know these cases are genuine, I still refuse to be certain. They are presented to me, under hypnosis, as a form of reincarnation, and the subjects who undergo them insist that they have been experiencing the life of another person. To that extent, as I have no more explanations to offer, I must accept that reincarnation is the only theory which can explain how a death can be recalled under hypnosis and, indeed, how the regression can be conducted in such fantastic detail. Now, I can do no more than recount them.

Q: 'Hello. What's your name?'
A: 'Kitty.'
Q: 'How old are you, Kitty?'
A: 'I'm ten.'
Q: 'And where do you live?'
A: 'Oh – big building.'
Q: 'What's your mummy's name? Have you got a mother?'
A: 'Haven't got one.'
Q: 'What town are you in?'
A: 'It's in Devon.'
Q: 'What do they say is the name of the village?'
A: ' 'Tis Chaggieford.'
Q: 'And what do you do all day?'
A: 'I have to work.'
Q: 'What kind of work?'
A: 'I be in the scullery.'
Q: 'What do you do in there?'
A: 'I have to clean.'
Q: 'Who owns this place?'
A: 'The Master.'

These were some of the first facts we learned about the sad life of Kitty Jay. Pauline, a nurse from Cheshire, gradually revealed her story under hypnosis, and it is one of the most remarkable I have ever heard.

We discovered that Kitty's surname was Jay and that she was an orphan living a life of some hardship. Jay was a name commonly given to illegitimate children in the eighteenth and nineteenth centuries, so instead we had to work on the town she had given us: Chaggieford. In Devon there is a town on the edge of Dartmoor called Chagford, which in the past has sometimes been referred to in the local records as Chaggieford. The librarian of Newton Abbot, the nearest large town, informed us that there was a legend of Jay's Grave, a lonely mound situated at the meeting of three roads on the edge of Dartmoor. (Suicides used to be buried at a crossroads, so that the ghost would not know which way to return to haunt the living; they were also not allowed to be buried on consecrated ground.)

The legend of Kitty Jay has been written up in newspapers, and in a book by Lois Deacon, *An Angel From Your Door*. It was the subject of much correspondence in the *Western Morning News* during the 1930s; one report from the time said: 'Mary Jay was a poor little workhouse apprentice who was hired out by the parish to a farmer living at Barracot Farm, near Manaton. One sad day she took a rope, went to a big barn belonging to Ford Farm near by, and hanged herself.'

Lois Deacon's book states that Kitty Jay was apprenticed at Ford Farm and hanged herself on a beam over a hearth of a disused ancient farmhouse called Canna Farm. Other accounts say she hanged herself at Wingstone, and that her name was Jane, or Betsy, or Mary. In other words, the stories surrounding this legend conflict with each other on some of the basic facts and differ wildly on peripheral details.

The fact that a legend existed naturally made us suspicious of this regression. Pauline could have picked up the story and then forgotten about it, only to relive it again under hypnosis. But this explanation had to be ruled out as the regression developed, for Pauline, as Kitty, developed a life story which contradicted or agreed with all the different versions at various stages, and also produced new information never previously recorded.

Q: 'Have you got any friends?'
A: 'Jamie.'

Q: 'Is he younger than you?'
A: 'Bigger than me.'
Q: 'What does Jamie call you?'
A: 'Kit.'
Q: 'Do you have another name?'
A: 'Mary.'
Q: 'Which comes first, Mary or Kit?'
A: 'Kitty.'

She began to produce information which only someone with a close knowledge of the period and the place could have known:

Q: 'Where is everyone today?'
A: 'Outside.'
Q: 'What are people doing outside?'
A: 'The men working.'
Q: 'What are they working at?'
A: 'They pick the oakum.'
Q: 'They pick the what?'
A: 'The oakum.'

Even more curious was the following:

Q: 'What happens to the old people when they die?'
A: 'They go to the kistvaens.'
Q: 'What are the kistvaens?'
A: 'They put the ash in.'

The word was unfamiliar to all of us, but the dictionary defined it as a burial chamber made of flat stones. At another session we put Pauline back to the first time she had ever heard the word 'kistvaen' during her own lifetime. She went back to the day of the regression when Kitty had first used the word.

From Kitty's descriptions of the 'big house', and the activities which seemed to be going on there, we assumed she must be in a workhouse. She gave a pitiful description of her surroundings, and of her friend Jamie:

Q: 'What are you doing today, Kitty?'
A: 'Go with the big lady.'
Q: 'Where?'
A: 'In the rooms.'
Q: 'And what do you do in the rooms with the big lady?'
A: 'We goes to people on the bed. She makes me stand and look.'
Q: 'What does she say?'
A: 'She says they go where mama goes.'
Q: 'What's wrong with the people, Kitty?'
A: 'They be poorly.'
Q: 'Who's there?'
A: 'Jamie.'
Q: 'How does he look?'
A: 'He do smell. Sores on his face. They do be a funny colour.'

Later we put Kitty forward and again asked her about Jamie:

Q: 'Where's Jamie?'
A: 'He's gone to the kistvaens.'

What we couldn't understand, however, was that, according to the records, there was no workhouse in Chagford; the various accounts of the legend managed to avoid the question or were vague on the issue, but Pauline was specific about the conditions in which Kitty was living. It was only two years later that one of the researchers found some old records of Chaggieford, brochures and booklets which were in such bad condition that they were not put on general display. They stated that there had been a house for the very elderly, run by the church authorities, where they also cared for illegitimate children. We asked Kitty if she ever had to go to church:

A: 'I go with the old cronies to St Mary's in Chaggieford.'

Again, the records show no sign of a church called St Mary's; but by chance our researcher, when talking to a ninety-year-old woman in the town, was shown a leaflet advertising a fête held by St Mary's Chapel.

Kitty was obviously unhappy at the big house. She told us that in the day she was sent off to work at a farm, for which she received some wages:

Q: 'Where's the master's farm, the master that you work for?'
A: ' 'Tis in Manaton.'
Q: 'What do you spend your wages on, Kitty?'
A: 'I keeps it.'
Q: 'What do you intend to do with it?'
A: 'I think I be running away.'

Then we found out about Rob, a local boy she had fallen in love with. We also heard more specific details of her surroundings:

A: 'He says I'm pretty.'
Q: 'Does he? And do you go walking with him?'
A: 'Aye.'
Q: 'And where do you go?'
A: 'We go to the bridge.'
Q: 'And where else?'
A: 'We sits by the stones.'
Q: 'By what stones?'
A: 'On the common.'
Q: 'Are they very old stones?'
A: 'They be big. They be in a ring.'
Q: 'What's the name of the farm where Rob works?'
A: 'Canna.'
Q: 'Tell me, if you want to go to Chaggieford, where do you go? Do you go down to the main road?'

A: 'I go across the fields.'
Q: 'Is there a lord of the manor?'
A: 'I knows of one.'
Q: 'What's his name?'
A: 'Sir John.'
Q: 'Sir John what?'
A: 'Whiddon.'
Q: 'Sir John Whiddon. How do you know him?'
A: 'I heard Rob say.'

At last we came to the time when Kitty had decided to cut her losses and run away. It seemed she was relying on Rob.

Q: 'What are you going to do?'
A: 'He said he'd meet me.'
Q: 'Where?'
A: 'At an old house. It's empty. We're going there. 'Tis an old farm.'
Q: 'Have you been there before?'
A: 'Nay. Rob knows.'
Q: 'So he is running away too?'
A: 'Oh, he be running away, aye.'

Soon, she was at the house.

Q: 'Where are you, Kitty?'
A: 'A house.'
Q: 'Are you alone?'
A: 'Nay.'
Q: 'Who is with you?'
A: 'Rob.'
Q: 'What's he doing?'
A: [She begins to look frightened.] 'He's trying to undress me. Rob ... don't do this ... Rob ... no, no ... please ...'

The first time we reached this point, Pauline became so

distressed we had to rouse her from hypnosis. She insisted, however, on going back to that moment, and there was no mistaking what had happened. It seemed this was a turning point in her relations with Rob.

Q: 'Hello, Kitty. Where's Rob?'
A: 'I think he do be going back.'
Q: 'What are you going to do?'
A: 'I'm alone here. Nobody here.'
Q: 'Why has he suddenly changed his mind?'
A: 'I wouldn't be knowing.'
Q: 'Haven't you asked him?'
A: 'He's different.'
Q: 'What's he saying then?'
A: 'He's going to go and leave me. He be going to leave me in the dark.'
Q: 'Why is he saying that?'
A: 'I'm cold.'
Q: 'Can't you go back?'
A: ' 'Tis too far to walk.'
Q: 'Would you think of going back tomorrow?'
A: 'I be thrashed.'

Later the situation worsened:

Q: 'What's the matter, Kitty?'
A: 'I'm looking for Rob.'
Q: 'Have you lost him?'
A: 'Aye.'
Q: 'For how long?'
A: 'For weeks.'
Q: 'Why's that?'
A: 'I don't know.'
Q: 'Has he been round to the barn?'
A: 'I ran away.'
Q: 'Where have you gone to?'

A: 'I've gone to an old place.'
Q: 'Where is it?'
A: 'Near Manaton.'
Q: 'What are you doing for food?'
A: 'I steal it.'
Q: 'Where do you steal it from?'
A: 'I went back to the farm.'
Q: 'Did you ask for food?'
A: 'They tell me to go away. They said I was a filthy wench.'

Raised in terrible conditions amongst sick old people, sent to work on a neighbouring farm, abandoned by a man who promised to run away with her, scavenging for food in the fields and stealing from farms, rejected by her employer even though she must have looked in a desperate state ... There was one last surprise to come: Kitty was pregnant.

A: 'Must go to Canna ... Must find Rob ... Must tell him ... 'Tis him who did it.'
Q: 'Have you seen him since that day?'
A: 'Nay.'
Q: 'Do you know when he left the farm?'
A: 'Nay.'

Then, when she failed to find him, her will seemed to break:

Q: 'Where are you?'
A: 'I'm going to the barn.'
Q: 'What are you going to do?'
A: 'Get rid of the baby.'
Q: 'How?'
A: 'With a rope. I'm going to kill myself. I'm so tired. 'Tis such a waste. My tummy is so big.'
Q: 'Where are you going to tie it?'
A: 'The beam.'
Q: 'Have you put it around your neck?'

A: 'Not yet.'
Q: 'Why not?'
A: 'I'm afraid. Nobody'll help.'
Q: 'Why kill yourself just because you're having a baby?'
A: 'Nobody can look after it.'
Q: 'Don't do it, Kitty. You can change your mind.'
A: 'No! I'm gonna jump, I'm gonna jump, I'm gonna jump ...'
A: 'Off to sleep, Kitty, drift off to sleep, Kitty, off to sleep ...'

This is how we learned of the death of Kitty Jay. Others may have learned of it from books and articles – and if they have read several, they will have come across conflicting reports – but to those present at these regression sessions there could be no doubt that the truth had been heard. It was a tragic and pitiful scene.

The case has not been without its share of mysteries. In about 1861 a Mr James Bryant of Hedge Barton had the grave which is said to be that of Kitty Jay opened and examined. He found the skeleton of a young woman, and as there was no proof as to the date of the girl's death, he had the bones placed in a box and re-interred on the spot where they had been found. A mound was raised, and the stones which lie there still were placed around it. To this day, flowers have always been found on Kitty's grave, and yet no one has ever been seen to place them there.

It is as if some family had felt obliged to do penance for the suffering a son had caused a poor young orphan girl.

Pauline's regression experiences have been the subject of several television and newspaper reports. One television company took her to a number of farms in the locality in Devon, the first time in fact that she had ever been to the area. At the first four farms, she showed no signs of any alarm and was quite happy strolling around the yard. At the fifth she became upset and actually refused to go any further.

The fifth was the site of Canna Farm.

There was an even stranger occurrence during the course of

Pauline's regressions. One morning, when she came downstairs, she found this written on the notepad at the side of her telephone:

Agan tas-ny, us yn nef,
Benygys re bo dha Hanow,
Re dheffo dha wlascor,
Dha voth re bo gwres, yn nor keper hag y'nnef
Ro dhyn – ny hedhyu agan bara detholl,
Ha gaf dhyn agan tamwyth
Kepar del aven-nyny dhe'n ve-na us ow
Camwul er agan pyn-ny
Hana wra agan gorra ya temptasyar
Mes delyrf ny dyworth drok
Rag dhyso-jy yu an wlascor ha'n
Gallos. ha'an gordnyans
Bys vyken ha bynary.

The handwriting was larger, less mature than Pauline's, and at first she was at a loss to explain how the strange message had appeared during the night. She had no idea what it meant, and nor did anyone in our group. Even when she realized that the handwriting must have been her own, but written *while she was sleepwalking*, she still could not explain its contents. .

We contacted the language department of Liverpool University and were put on to Professor Nicholas Williams of University College, Dublin, the Head of the Celtic Department at Liverpool from 1974 to 1977. He recognized the script immediately: 'You enclosed, quite simply, a transcript of the Lord's Prayer in "revised" Cornish. Cornish became extinct at the end of the eighteenth century. This century, the revivalists have used a regularized spelling and have adopted the medieval form of the language. Although no one speaks Cornish natively, it is gaining some currency as a language for enthusiasts, nationalists and so forth.'

Why should Pauline have written out the Lord's Prayer in

Cornish – and revised Cornish at that – during her sleep? Kitty had no connection that we know of with Cornwall, and neither does Pauline herself have any knowledge of the language. It is almost as though her regression experiences of the short and unhappy life of Kitty Jay had opened up some mysterious filter in her subconscious mind, allowing other elements to reach through. If so, to what set of memories can this Cornish Lord's Prayer be attached? Could it be any more astounding than that we have already witnessed?

Pauline's case, like all those in this chapter, seems to point firmly in the direction of reincarnation. The details of her regressions, the accuracy of her accounts – surely no other explanation can make sense of what went on in those sessions? Perhaps the case of Cliff Pattinson can shed more light …

Cliff first regressed to a boy called Jim Jackson, the son of a blacksmith on a large estate in Ainderby Steeple, in North Yorkshire. Jim was afflicted with what he called 'the palsy' (loss of motion and muscular control), which stopped him attending school or taking part in any of the activities of other boys around him. When he was well enough, he helped in the squire's stables.

Under questioning, Jim insisted that he never went to church. We were sure that he must at least know the name of a local church, by which we might identify the area and period more closely, but the name of the church Jim gave us seemed not to exist. After considerable research, however, we discovered that the preacher mentioned by Jim – a Mr Hirst – had lived and worked in Ainderby Steeple, at a chapel with the same name supplied by Jim.

Somehow Cliff knew facts which it had taken us hours and weeks to uncover. But not just these facts. Judy Sissons, a librarian in Huddersfield, conducted much of the research for this regression, and she takes up the story:

> While researching this regression, I chanced upon a mine of information in the form of an old book, kept in the stack at Leeds

Reference Library, called *On Sea and Shore* by Thomas Hedger. Published in the late nineteenth century, it is the reminiscences of this seafaring gentleman who spent the first thirteen years of his life in Ainderby Steeple, a few years earlier than Jim Jackson, the character to whom Cliff regresses.

Armed with obscure information culled from this dusty old book, at the next regression group Joe Keeton first put Cliff through his own life to any time he had heard or read anything about Thomas Hedger. Then to any time he was reading *On Sea and Shore*. There was no trace of Cliff's ever having heard of either.

During Cliff's regression to Jim, I questioned him using the names of people taken from the book, all of whom Jim should have known about.

First of all, we asked about 'Peggy w't airm' (Peggy without an arm); this is how everyone in the village referred to Margaret Miller, a woman who had had one of her arms amputated just below the shoulder due to injuries received from a threshing machine. He replied that he knew of her and seemed to think that she had had her arm taken off in an accident with a wheel. Naturally we were disappointed that he did not make a specific mention of the threshing machine, but consoled ourselves with the fact that a rather solitary young lad with the palsy who preferred horses to people – or girls, at any rate – possibly wouldn't be very good on details.

After some general chatter, we tried again. Someone asked Jim if he knew Rachel, giving him no information other than the name. Yes, he did know 'Spike Rachel', as he called her, and he didn't much like her, despite the fact that she made sweets and did a 'bit of baking'. She also made baskets. The book tells us that Rachel was known as 'Spice Rachel'. She was the wife of the village basketmaker and supplied the village children with toffee.

We decided to try Jim with another formidable female; did he know 'Butcher Dolly'? Yes, he did: unfortunately the only detail he was able to provide us with is not verifiable from the book, but it is certainly in character with what we know of the village of Ainderby Steeple at the time. 'She swipes at t'bloody butcher when he's drunk,' he said.

Jim was sent to a time when he recognized the names George Calvert and/or Neddy Henderson. These young men were both regular winners of the customary race run by the youths of the village whenever there was a wedding. When we could see from the rapid eye movement that at least one of these names had evoked some memories, we asked if he knew anything about either of these people. He mentioned the name of one and said that he was a good runner.

This questioning on customs and people of the village continued for two hours. Jim was eighty per cent accurate all the time.

I consider memories such as these, concerning very ordinary people rather than the lord of the manor, or other gentry, to be very important in establishing the genuineness or otherwise of a regression.

We could never get the squire's name from Jim. Despite insistent questioning, all he ever called him was simply that – 'the Squire'.

Take for example Neddy Henderson and George Calvert. Those names could have belonged to the butcher, the baker or the candlestickmaker; to match them straight away to a person who was a good runner is a far from obvious step to take. Had Cliff been fantasizing the whole regression, he would most likely have attributed the name to some village tradesman or other. As it was, he attributed them correctly, providing us with yet another piece of evidence that, despite our being unable to find him on the census forms, a lad with the palsy called Jim did live in Ainderby Steeple during the first half of the nineteenth century.

Cliff went on to regress to a second character under hypnosis. This was a little girl called Emma, who lived in Reading. She told us that her father was 'something to do with the law' and that his name was Robertson. They lived in St Bartholomews Road.

The Kelly's and Smith's directories of Reading for the years 1888–95 list a William Henry Robertson as living at 4 Fatherson

Road, 36 Cholemeley Road (from 1891) and 44 Cholemeley Road (from 1894). Early entries describe him as an 'Inspector of Nuisances', later ones as 'Sanitary Inspector'; whether this was a promotion or simply a change in terminology is not really of any relevance here. Now, although there is no trace of any Robertsons living in St Bartholomews Road itself, both Cholemeley Road and Fatherson Road are in the area known as St Bartholomews.

Emma must have had her leg pulled unmercifully at school, because when we taxed her with the fact that her father was a 'bug-catcher', she burst into tears and took a lot of consoling. She must have spent a lot of time covering up for what she considered an embarrassing job for her father to do.

Cliff himself has never been to Reading, and knows nothing at all about the layout of the town. In fact, there have been many changes to it since the last century, and it was not too hard to check the memories of the town that Cliff produced as Emma. For example, any time she was at the addresses in Cholemeley Road, she described the houses very accurately.

In an early regression Emma mentioned a biscuit shop owned by a Mr Huntley. Asked about Mr Palmer, she replied that she had no knowledge of him at all. Consciously, Cliff must have heard of Huntley & Palmers the biscuitmakers, but when regressed to Emma he had no idea what we were talking about. Then we brought him forward a few years and asked about the biscuit shop. Emma said that there was a factory nearby owned by Huntley and a man named Palmer. The now-famous Huntley & Palmer biscuit factory is situated in the St Bartholomews area of Reading, in King's Road North.

We took some names at random from the directories and suggested to Emma that her memories should drift to any time when she was in a place owned by Susan and Sarah Cook. Emma said she was in Castle Street and had come for her hatbox. Our directories showed that the Cook sisters were milliners at 33 Castle Street.

The Power of the Mind

Using the same technique, we asked Emma to go to any memories of when she might have bought a basket. She said she was in Cooks' shop in the market-place. The directories show that the Cooks were basketmakers and that they were situated at 11 High Street, next door to the market site.

For someone who has never been to the town, Cliff's answers to a long series of questions about the geography of the city, including old street names and alterations to buildings, is nothing short of extraordinary.

Most of the regressions described in this book have concerned the lives of ordinary men and women, and often children, who by the very normality of their existence seem somehow to make the case for reincarnation more acceptable. There is no grand story-telling, no extravagant tales, just the honest portrayal of how lives must have been led in the past. But once, just once, a well-known historical character emerged from a regression in such an authentic way that it seemed we really had stumbled upon a famous past life.

The person was Nell Gwynn, a name so familiar to everyone that, when she first appeared during a session, we assumed this to be no more than a familiar fantasy, another example of the ever-inventive unconscious at work. But as time went on, our certainty began to falter, for Edna G, an elderly Lancashire housewife, produced almost a hundred hours of regressions in the character of Nell Gwynn, the orange-seller who became the mistress of Charles II. And no matter how hard we tried, we could not trick her into revealing that her regression was a fantasy or a fraud.

We regressed Edna to Nell for several hours at a time. We switched her from year to year, from incident to incident, backwards and forwards like the pendulum of a great clock, but without the clock's regularity or predictability. During these marathon sessions, time would stand still for a moment, then race clockwise or anticlockwise like the mechanism of a timepiece gone awry. But every time the clock in Edna's head proved correct – she never made a mistake, in almost a hundred hours. It was an uncanny experience.

Nell was of course an actress as well as an orange-seller, but the answers she gave to some of our questions about her acting were not as we might have expected. For example, when we questioned her about specific plays in which we knew she had taken part, she usually gave the second or sub-title, rather than the name by which the play had subsequently become known. She mentioned having appeared in *The Maiden Queen*, whereas the title page actually reads *Secret Love, or the Maiden Queen*. Nell was no scholar, and her memory of titles seems somewhat sketchy:

A: 'I were in Eighty Days ... or Eighty Years ... I've forgot.'
Q: 'Who was the author of that?'
A: 'Not right sure. Don't know whether it were Dryden, or Killigrew, or ... who's that other one? Oh, Bucks ... he tried to write something.'

The play she was trying to remember was probably *Queen Elizabeth's Tragedy, or the History of Eighty-Eight* by Thomas Heywood. Again, it was the subtitle which had stuck in her memory.

The real Nell Gwynn was a heavy drinker, like most of the Court of Charles II, and there is no doubt that Edna, when regressed to Nell, often showed all the signs of drunkenness. But what is most fascinating is that, during all the hours she spent under hypnosis, Edna, who has only a slight education herself, was able to produce an incredible amount of verifiable historical detail. She even gave us facts which have yet not yet been traced, such as the names of the spaniels owned by Charles II. Can it really be true that we were witnessing the memories of Nell Gwynn, or is there another explanation? What seems certain is that Edna was not faking or lying, as her next regression was to show.

Jenny Preston was one of the lesser-known Lancashire witches who lived on the bleak, windswept moors in the shadow of Pendle Hill during the seventeenth century. When regressed to Jenny, Edna took on all the tones and mannerisms of the ghastly woman but, more significantly, contradicted the lurid and somewhat inconsistent account of the witches' trial written by Pott. The actual transcripts of the trial are lost at present, so we cannot confirm Edna's account; what we can do is show how she manages to produce information about Jenny which seems to put Pott quite in the wrong.

Pott said that Jenny had been tried and hanged at York some time before the famous and well-documented Lancashire trials. Edna insisted that Jenny had been tortured and then released at York. Evidence shows that Jenny was indeed questioned at the subsequent Lancashire trials, so it would seem Edna is correct and Pott is wrong. Similarly, Edna always insisted that Jenny had lived in Gisburn, and it was only by chance that one of our researchers met an old man in Gisburn (close to Clitheroe, the scene of the witches' tale) who confirmed that local lore had it that Jenny Preston had lived in the town.

Reincarnation or fantasy? It is probably too early to tell, because new information may still come to light confirming or denying Edna's regression. In the case of Frances Isaacson, the case for reincarnation may be a little clearer.

Frances is a sixty-year-old craft teacher who lives in Seattle in the USA. She had already regressed to two American personalities when a further regression seemed to draw a blank: she could not understand what we were saying. Her daughter then mentioned that Frances' grandparents had been Scandinavian immigrants, and that it might be worth questioning her in Swedish. The response was immediate:

Q: '*Och vad heter du?*' ('What is your name?')
A: '*Anna.*'
Q: '*Anna ... Vad da dista namet?*' ('What is your last name?')
A: '*Karlsson.*'
Q: '*Ah ... Anna Karlsson.*'
A: (She nodded.): '*Trevligt att traffas.*' ('How do you do')

As we progressed, Anna's fluency increased, and she began to talk animatedly in Swedish. At first we thought this must be firm proof for the theory of reincarnation, for if an English-speaking person stops being able to speak English under hypnosis and instead understands only Swedish, she must be recalling the memories of someone other than herself. As it turned out, Frances had apparently been spoken to only in Swedish for the first six months of her life, so it is possible that under hypnosis her unconscious mind recalled all the Swedish she had ever heard during those six months, and so constructed a fantasy in Swedish about Anna Karlsson. (In fact, some relatives of Frances wrote from Sweden to confirm that an Anna Karlsson had lived in the area she had stated under regression, and in the same period.) Again, we cannot tell, but both Frances' and Edna's stories give us cause to consider the case for reincarnation.*

Ultimately, of course, there is no definite answer, and the search for knowledge goes on. We may be dealing in some of the most fantastic and unsettling regions of human experience, but there is still no substitute for patient and methodical research. I myself have conducted countless regression sessions over the years, but every time I utter the words, 'You are going back ...', I still wait with apprehension for the response, because I never know where it will take us: to the life of some untraceable child, left to fend for itself in the harsh world of the nineteenth-century city; to the story of a woman and her family, living and loving in an eighteenth-century village; to the confessions of a soldier, hardened by the tough realities of war in years gone by. Each story has its own quality of wonder, and while we may try to come to an understanding of the links between the past and the present which we are witnessing, we are also struck by the utter mystery before our eyes.

One thing we can be sure of: I, along with countless others,

* They are both recounted at length in *Encounters With the Past* by Peter Moss and myself, published by Sidgwick & Jackson in hardback, and Penguin in paperback.

have seen the past, have listened to history and can tell of events before my time. It is an insight open to all of us but exercised still by comparatively few. But as more and more participate and observe, so our knowledge will grow and so our experience of life and of ourselves will deepen. Surely there could be no greater aim.

5   Physical Healing

The one firm conclusion that we can draw from our experience of hypnotic regression, the one certainty which arises from such an accumulation of remarkable detail, is this: we know very little about our own minds. As a civilization we may have progressed in many fields, but we cannot claim much success in understanding our potential.

All those who have come into contact with regression go away with a new perspective on the workings of the mind. They know that they can never again be complacent, and they also know that it will be a long time before they even begin to come to terms with the mysteries they have uncovered. When faced with some of the experiences witnessed in the last chapter, such a reaction is not surprising. But we should not be deterred from the long process of exploration simply because the facts which we discover threaten the equilibrium of our present understanding.

In fact, hypnosis and hypnotic regression have opened up a whole new way of considering the question of health. And unlike the cases described in the last chapter, which are often open to several explanations, the examples we shall be looking at in this chapter are irrefutable. They can be examined and tested under any conditions and can be proved to arise directly from the benefits obtained through hypnosis. Since we know that physical healing can be effected in this way, we need now to analyse the physical processes by which the mind controls the body. Once we understand that, we will have moved on to a new generation of medicine and health.

We could be very close to such a discovery. We are certainly too close to turn back.

Evolution and the mind

For about 4,000 million years, mankind has been engaged in one of the cruellest, most ruthless games of all. 'Evolution' is the term we use to describe what is otherwise known as 'the survival of the fittest', and it means just that. Nothing that is too weak for its environment has been allowed to survive on this planet, and only those creatures which have successfully adapted to change have reproduced in sufficient quantities to safeguard their race.

Whether we like it or not, we are part of that terrible contest. Our ancestors have been strong, quick and resilient, and they have bequeathed to us their survival instinct. Modern urban man may bear little outward resemblance to the hunter of long ago, but he is still a man all the same. He no longer has to live in the wilds, naked to the wind and rain, so he is no longer protected by such a thick coating of hair as before. He no longer has to fight and kill for his food, so his physique has adapted, his arms losing their power. During this gradual process of change, has he lost some of the strengths which he still needs?

Earlier in the book, we looked at the various types of relaxation which are possible, and mentioned the way a cat or a dog is able to curl up and sleep at will, at any time during the day. While it is asleep, the slightest unusual sound – too faint for a human ear to hear – will waken it and put it on its guard. It seems that babies, before their parents train them to sleep only at night, are capable of the same 'instant sleep', and that this ability is lost by being discouraged.

It is my belief that this loss accounts for many of the ills we encounter later in life. During this kind of sleep, the mind is relaxed but watched over by the unconscious. Back in the times when we were hunters, we needed to be able to relax but still, like an animal, spring into action at the slightest warning of danger. Now, despite our comfortable surroundings, we still need to use our unconscious minds, because, as regression has shown, they are capable of far more than we imagine.

During sleep, the unconscious mind looks out for us. It ignores unthreatening sounds such as traffic and the wind, but the slightest unfamiliar noise can often waken us immediately. Without consulting the conscious mind, it decides the possibility of danger is too great to ignore. So not only does it control our breathing patterns, it also takes decisions. When we are awake, too, the unconscious has a role. When fear reaches a certain level, it authorizes the production of adrenalin. In the *Guinness Book of Records* is an account of an old woman whose grandson was knocked down by a car, which came to rest with the front wheels on his legs. Without the use of a jack or any other form of assistance, the grandmother lifted the car for long enough to allow the boy to escape.

Other, less startling achievements of the unconscious may be witnessed every day. People who make a regular car journey – for example, from home to work – often find that they have covered several miles without realizing it. They may arrive at work and have no memory of the journey they have just taken, perhaps because they were worrying about a pressing problem, or daydreaming. And yet if they drove that journey while concentrating, they would constantly be aware of details they had to consider, such as another car driving a little too close, or the traffic lights changing at an inconvenient moment. How can they cope with such details if their conscious mind is thinking about something entirely different and is concentrating on this so much that it later has no memory of driving at all? The answer, of course, is that the unconscious mind takes over, carrying out the normal functions of driving and calling back the conscious mind into control if an emergency arises.

What power is there, just waiting to be harnessed! Think of a normal day, and try to picture how often you rely upon the unconscious when your conscious mind is occupied with something else. Involuntarily, the unconscious comes to your aid every day, every hour. But it is an 'automatic' function, it is not something you deliberately set into motion yourself. This is one of the strengths we lack and which hypnosis is able to recover. For by learning how to relax oneself into a hypnotic state, the unconscious can be brought to bear far more often, and far more effectively, than it normally is.

In the days when we had no medicine, when we killed and hunted to survive, we had no choice when it came to illness: either we recovered of our own accord or we died. If modern man, with all his cleanliness and germ-free living, was transposed into such an environment, he would collapse very quickly. Even now, when we are given an inoculation against smallpox – which teaches the body how to produce the necessary antibody to combat infection – the inoculation wears off after about five years. The body 'forgets' its instruction and reverts to being susceptible to the smallpox infection.

It seems we have evolved into a species that is unable to protect itself from disease. Where before our bodies would have attempted to deal with a problem, now we rely on a drug to do the work for us. The antiseptic lifestyle so many of us have adopted has, ironically, left us more prone to disease than before. As I hope to show in this chapter, we still have the chance to recover those immunity systems because like so much that we do not understand, those systems are locked away in our unconscious minds. Just as we are the same species as the hunter of thousands of millions of years ago, so we retain the same knowledge, inherited in our unconscious just by virtue of being human. From generation to generation, the ability to resist disease has been passed on. Unless we take some action soon, we could be in danger of losing that resistance in a flood of pills, tablets and injections.

Stress, pain and modern medicine

Stress is probably the greatest killer in the world today. It contributes to coronary disease, cancer and many other illnesses too numerous to mention. It can result from many different factors, from overwork to emotional disturbance, from unsuitable living conditions to difficult personal relations. Its effect can be devastating, and the variety of illnesses it can result in limitless.

The next time you visit a zoo, go to the enclosures where

several animals of the same species are kept together. Leaving apart the very young, how easy is it to tell a two-year-old from a nine-year-old? Now think of all the friends you have who are over sixty, the equivalent of a nine-year-old in animal terms. Some of them will look more like fifty, some more like seventy. It is stress, or the absence of it, which is at the root of those physiological differences. A stressful life will, as they say, put years on you.

When our bodies are functioning properly, we remove all the stresses which have accumulated during the day. If you wake up as tired as you were before you went to bed, you are failing to remove the tensions within you and in fact are allowing them to take root. If you allow those tensions to remain and to be built upon every day, you are setting into motion a cycle of stress which will attack both the body and the mind. The key to unlocking it lies in the unconscious mind, by achieving a state of true hypnosis and relaxing.

Later in this chapter we will be looking at many examples of what we call 'illnesses' or 'diseases' and showing how they may be eliminated by tackling the conditions of stress which produce them. Hypnosis, unlike other methods, such as meditation, which achieve only a slight and temporary form of relaxation, is the only real solution to stress of this kind. We know, for example, that a head can 'ache' only in a special sense; there is certainly no bruising of the brain during a headache, no damaging of the cranium. The ache which we feel is usually the direct result of some form of stress, and it is only through using the healing, relaxing powers of the unconscious that we may rid ourselves of the pain.

If the idea of removing headaches by relaxation seems difficult to accept, consider what the body is able to do automatically under conditions of extreme pain. The unconscious stimulates the production of a substance known as endorphines, which act in the same way as morphine to remove pain. As a child, I would deal with toothache by hitting the offending tooth hard with my knuckles. The pain this caused was sharp and intense, but the actual toothache disappeared for some time, because the endorphines I had caused to be released were acting as a drug on my senses. People who have been shot say that they felt no real pain until some hours after, when the initial rush of endorphines had run its course. A mother was able to dash into a burning house to rescue her children, feeling no pain from the terrible burns for which she later had to be treated.

This mechanism is normally brought into play only in extreme circumstances. Hypnosis, by allowing access to the unconscious, lets you employ it at will. It gives you control over the pain which you experience and, like the hunter of before, allows you to continue until you reach safety.

Compare this method with our usual one of taking drugs. I quote from an advertisement for a pain-killing drug routinely prescribed by doctors: 'Power over pain ... Recommended starting dose, one gram a day.' Then came the small print:

> Side effects: Digestive system: gastric pain, dyspepsia, anorexia, nausea, vomiting, constipation, diarrhoea, flatulence, eructation. Isolated cases of gastro-intestinal ulcers and bleeding. Central nervous system: vertigo, somnolence, headache, insomnia, dizziness, fatigue, tiredness, transient visual disturbances, paraesthesia, depression, nervousness, tinnitus. Skin: pruritus, rash, sweating, dry mucous membranes and stomatitis. Cross-sensitivity with aspirin suspected in two cases. A few cases of erythema multiforme, including Stevens-Johnson syndrome reported; causal relationship not established. Miscellaneous: oedema, dyspnoea, palpitation, syncope, muscle cramps, dysuria, fever, malaise, hypersensitivity, anaphylactic reaction with broncospasm.

Another advertisement for a drug says that it 'lets hypersensitives live life to the full' but then in small print warns that, 'Bradycardia and heart failure may occur during therapy.'

What kind of medicine is it that allows for the possibility of creating further, often more severe problems during therapy? Obviously the side-effects quoted above develop in only some patients, and then it is only one or two, not the whole list of illnesses the drug company provides. But still, many people suffer unnecessarily because they use artificially created pain-killers instead of relying on their own bodies' immune systems. All drugs that the body needs can be produced by the body itself without any external interference, just as it has been for millions of years. By taking manufactured drugs, we are losing our innate ability to allow our own biological systems to function.

Through hypnosis, most of us can learn how to control pain, whether it is stress-related or the result of injury. Once we have learned the technique, it is vital that we use it sensibly. The pain from a broken limb may be controlled, but we still need to get to a hospital to have it reset; the pain which can be controlled but which keeps coming back is a warning that something is wrong with our body which needs examining by a doctor: migraine headaches can be conquered, but the worry, unhappiness or fear which is causing them still needs to be faced. And, of course, medical treatment which duplicates the body's own protective substances, such as insulin for the treatment of diabetes, cannot be replaced by hypnosis.

But the potential is there, within each and every one of us, for the relief of suffering which we consider treatable only by dangerous drugs. Most of us shrink from the thought of heroin abuse or cocaine addiction; why do we abuse ourselves in just the same way with drugs that come in labelled bottles?

Over the years I have shown many people how to take control of their lives by gaining control of their bodies. Here are the testimonies of some …

Andrew Selby has found many uses for his newly-found ability to harness the power of his unconscious mind. Using the relaxation techniques I have taught him, he is able to put himself into a state of hypnosis and has had good cause to employ his own natural pain-killing method.

I was taking part in a gymnastic class at a leisure centre in

London, and with the assistance of two instructors was attempting a back somersault.

I landed awkwardly, with one leg on top of the other, on the mat. Feeling the bone in my leg snap, I immediately turned off the pain as I had been taught, to such good effect that the teachers did not believe the leg was broken until the chief instructor actually felt the fracture. I obviously experienced the discomfort of the displaced bones and any attempt at moving the leg brought back the pain, making it necessary to keep repeating the pain removal. While I kept the leg still, there was just a feeling of uneasiness and frustration.

Throughout my stay in the hospital, including when the leg was being set, I took no artificial pain-killers whatsoever. Whether or not the doctors and nurses thought I was a masochist or a stoic, I neither know nor care.

After the plaster had been put on my leg and X-rays had been taken, I was told that it was a ninety per cent certainty that I would have to have my leg pinned. I had a bad fracture of the tibia and fibula, known as Pott's Fracture. This is a break across the lower end of the tibia (shinbone) and the fibula (the two long bones between the knee and the ankle). At the same time the ankle joint is dislocated. It is a very common injury which is usually treated by manipulation under general anaesthesia, followed by immobilization in a plaster cast for weeks. Sometimes the broken bones are operated on to try to pin them together. It is named after the surgeon Percival Pott who, while recovering from the condition, wrote the first complete text on it.

After examining the second X-ray, taken a few days later, the doctor decided pinning of the fracture was unnecessary, since the leg was healing itself so efficiently.

My leg was in plaster for thirteen weeks, though I felt no pain. The first night in the plaster was very uncomfortable, but after that I felt no discomfort at all.

When the plaster was removed, I worked on my leg, using both self-hypnosis and exercises recommended by the physiotherapist, with the result that two weeks later I was able to walk in to the doctor and hand him my crutches. I no longer needed them.

In the four years since the accident, I have felt no pain in the joints of the leg, and am not inhibited in any way by any after effects. My leg is as good as it ever was.

Joan illustrates another side to the use of hypnosis:

For seven years I had suffered from pain and stiffness in my neck. Movement was restricted and I was unable to turn my head round beyond a certain point.

Visits to my GP resulted in the diagnosis of arthritis, but I received no treatment for the condition.

I first met Joe Keeton because of my very great interest in psychology, and what he was doing seemed to me to come into that field of research.

I volunteered to sit in the chair and try for myself, not really expecting to go into the hypnotic state. I did, very quickly, but it seemed to be a shock to my whole system. I jumped almost out of the chair before I went into a state of complete relaxation.

Because of this unusual reaction, I was immediately roused, and questioned about what I felt. When I explained that every time I went to sleep that sort of thing happened and that to me it was a normal thing, the hypnosis was started again.

While under hypnosis I was given all the treatments that Joe, due to his experience, considered necessary to prepare me for regression. I was taught how to hypnotize myself, and my own immune systems were re-activated.

After this first session I turned to speak to someone behind me and, to my amazement, I realized that I was able to turn my head round, with no stiffness or pain. This happened 3½ years ago, and the trouble with my neck has not recurred.

This kind of recovery has been repeated countless times at my sessions, and I will include only a couple more at this point.

Anne suffered from tension, lack of sleep and chronic migraine for about twenty-five years. Now in her mid-forties and a housewife, she could not get through the day without tranquillizers and pain-killers, nor could she sleep at night without the assistance of drugs. She suffered from a variety of fears and phobias, the cause of which could not be determined by the doctors who treated her. It occurred to her, after contributing to a radio phone-in programme about hypnosis, that this form of therapy might be able to help her in some small way. She proved to be a perfect hypnotic subject and responded well to treatment – so well that, after a single session, she was able to control her attacks of migraine. Her tablet consumption dropped from eleven per day to none at all, and she felt healthier than she had since her childhood.

John Jones, a training assistant on the staff of the *Liverpool Post and Echo*, had experienced severe back pain for about ten years. He believed it had started with a slipped disc and, although X-ray tests proved negative, the pain and discomfort continued; his doctor explained that the condition was something he would 'just have to live with'.

In 1974 he visited an osteopath for a series of manipulative and heat treatments, after which his long-standing cramp disappeared. But he still suffered from back and shoulder pain, which was later aggravated by what his doctor diagnosed in 1976 as spinal arthritis. The pain in his back was regularly accompanied by pain in his shoulders and neck, and he found that without his medically prescribed anti-inflammatory tablets he could not even raise his arm. The only way he could sleep at night was with a hard board under his mattress, but this brought back the cramp in his legs.

Then, in 1979, he had hypnotherapy, a rather hurried treatment as he was just about to set off to Scotland on a motoring holiday. After returning, he said:

'Nothing seemed to have happened at first, but suddenly, after a few hours of driving, I felt a strange sensation in my back. It was as if something had clicked into position, and flexibility was restored to all the stiffened joints. I could move my head without any discomfort in my neck, and my spine appeared to be back to normal too. Since that moment, I have had no trouble at all. My toe joints used to be so stiff, but now I have a spring in my step again. It is great to be able to walk comfortably and without having to watch every move. I feel wonderful.'

A similar speedy reaction occurred with Mr D, who was suffering from a brain tumour. After coming to his first session with me, his wife wrote to me to say: 'Thank you for talking to my husband ... [he] came away feeling more positive and hopeful. ... At present [he] has come off prescribed valium and morphine, and also sleeps and rests peacefully without any pain. I must thank you again for your time and professionalism in treating my husband.'

The case of young Toby was complicated by the intervention of surgeons. Through hynotherapy I had helped him cure his spastic condition, but their work caused further damage. His father explained in a letter to me after the first treatment: 'Toby's condition is now cured but he is left with the legacy of misguided surgery in his left lower leg. He and I both feel that he could do much to regain full control of the limb if he could return to self-hypnosis. To this end, I would like to bring Toby to see you to "reactivate" him.'

While Toby's spasticity is now a thing of the past, we must begin the work of mending the unnecessary damage of surgery.

Rheumatism and similar complaints

Like most machines, our bodies use movable joints. An engineer would call them 'ball-and-socket' joints, with the ball-shaped part running inside the cup-shaped socket. As with engines, the joints of our bodies have to be kept greased, or oiled, if they are not to seize up and become static. Too little oil will cause excessive wear on the surface of each part; no oil at all will render the joint immobile.

There is a mechanism whereby our bodies produce and distribute the substance we need to keep all our joints supple and free from pain. It is initiated in the unconscious part of the brain, an operation over which the conscious mind has no control. This mechanism, when we are healthy, operates non-stop and ensures that just the right amount of fluid lubricant is supplied to each joint. You can imagine what a mess the conscious mind would make of such a job!

If something goes wrong with this mechanism and we stop producing the lubricant, the result is some form of rheumatic complaint. The longer the complaint is allowed to go on, the worse the seizing-up of the joints, and consequently the more painful the experience. It is at this point most sufferers go on to pain-killers, and thus embark upon that unfortunate dependency on dangerous and damaging chemicals.

Through hypnosis and the opening up of the unconscious mind, it is possible both to stem the pain caused by the inflamed joints, and to correct the malfunction of the whole lubricating mechanism.

Consider the case of Mrs Morley-Kirk:

During the mid-1970s I started to develop rheumatism in my knees. Within twelve to eighteen months this had spread to my ankles, elbows, wrists and fingers. To walk became extremely painful and also caused my knees to swell to easily twice their normal size.

My doctor gave me various pills to try and combat the rheumatism. Not only did these have very little effect, but they also gave me a seriously upset stomach. I eventually gave up taking the drugs as the pain was less discomfort than the stomach upsets.

My husband and I set about looking for alternatives. We visited Culpepper's, the herbalists in London, and I commenced a course of herbal preparations, which in fact did help a little.

During May 1980 my luck changed dramatically. My husband during a conversation with one of his business colleagues, mentioned my rheumatic problems and how he felt that before I had reached the age of forty-five I would end up being pushed for walks in a wheelchair. His colleague recalled that his son had suffered for years with eczema and that a man who lived near Liverpool had cured him, and had a reputation for helping with arthritis and similar complaints.

This seemed too good to be true, and it was not until the August of 1980 that I ventured to ring Mr Joe Keeton for an appointment. Only one visit was needed. The rest I did for myself in the way Joe Keeton taught me.

After approximately four to five weeks, sixty per cent of the pain and swellings had gone; the remainder took another five to six months to correct. I can now walk wherever I like, move my wrists and fingers perfectly without any fear of pain, and have no stiffness in any of my joints.

In Appendix B and Appendix C, Marjorie Bunyard and Brian Hitchen give their own accounts of their encounter with hypnotism and its contribution to healing. But there are many more who, like them, have rediscovered the vital truths about the human body which so often remain hidden from us. The fundamental truth is that, given the opportunity, the unconscious mind is capable of ministering to the body's problems, of controlling pain and of repairing the damage caused by bodily malfunctions. Stress is the primary factor blocking this unconscious activity, and stress can usually be dissolved by the relaxation methods of self-hypnosis. But if we are to make any progress, we must also accept that hypnosis can put us back in touch with the self-healing powers which once we all possessed.

Valerie gives a good example of the overall power of hypnosis:

Early in 1976, when I was thirty-six-years-old, I developed bracial neuralgia (severe pain in the arm) and other odd symptoms which my doctor attributed to arthritis.

I had intensive therapy for several months, then more tests and eventually complete bed rest in hospital. This was an attempt to relieve the pressure on the fifth, sixth and seventh cervical (neck) nerves. Finally, and reluctantly, my doctors decided to operate, although the odds were only 50/50.

The neuro-surgeon, on operating, found that I had a hairline fracture of a vertebra and blown-up discs, which had affected my central nervous system and compressed the median nerve. The operation was only partially successful – I still had intense pain in my right hand and shoulders.

My recovery was very slow: bed rest for nine months, then rehabilitation. After two years, and with my doctor's help, I regained my driving licence, with a specially adapted car (the licence renewable every three years because of my medical condition). Driving helped me to become more independent, but I needed help in running my home and caring for my children.

Four years later, after consulting many experts who all agreed that the median nerve was damaged and wouldn't recover, I heard Joe Keeton on a radio programme. He was talking about removing pain through hypnotherapy and, with my doctor's encouragement, I got in touch with him.

We met on 4 August 1980 and under hypnosis most of my pain disappeared, apart from the neuralgia in my right hand. At a small regression group a few days later, I saw Joe Keeton again and was introduced to someone who had severe arthritis and who used self-hypnosis to remove the pain.

I told myself that, if she could do it, then so could I and, as a man in the group was being hypnotized, I felt myself drifting along also. Very soon, the neuralgia in my hand slowed down and was gone. And then I was taught the technique of self-hypnosis for pain removal.

I cannot describe how it felt to be free from pain for the first time in four years. It is impossible to put my thoughts into words.

Since meeting Joe Keeton and using hypnosis, I have changed from a person who was very ill, needing bed rest, sleeping pills and pain-killers constantly, to someone who is physically very active and able to care for my home, family and dogs. The invalid sticker and special adaptations have been removed from my car. I am healthy and able-bodied again.

I do have occasional pain in my neck and hand, but it is usually when I am under stress and, provided I use self-hypnosis as taught, I am soon fine again.

Incidentally, I have not needed to consult my doctor about my neck since meeting Joe Keeton.

The one point I always emphasize when teaching people the technique of self-hypnosis is that, although it can be used to eradicate pain, it should not be used to ignore the warning that the pain is trying to give us. Pain should always be used as an alarm clock: when the clock rings, we turn it off and then take some action – such as getting up or taking a pie out of the oven. Pain too should be turned off, but we should always bear in mind what the body is trying to tell us by producing the pain in the first place. Perhaps it is trying to tell us that we are stressed, in which case we can resolve the problem by relaxation methods. But if the pain returns, the body is obviously warning us that something is wrong, and there should be no doubts about going straight to the doctor.

Self-hypnosis may be very effective as a healthy alternative to pain-killers, but it should never take the place of a medical examination. The examples of physical healing which we are considering in this chapter have almost always come *after* the medical profession has given up on a case – I do not presume to encroach on the skill and experience of doctors.

Hypnotherapy, regeneration and bodily malfunctions

We have already discussed the extraordinary process of evolution which has brought the human species to its present stage of development. The very process, as we have seen, has given us inherited strengths which we should be turning to our advantage. But my work in hypnotherapy has also taught me that the nine-month period in which a cell becomes a baby in a mother's womb also has great significance for our health.

The very first cell that starts off our lives begins, on fertilization, to multiply in the womb. First we resemble a sponge, but as development continues the first brain in the head is formed; it is known as the 'fish' brain. At this stage we have gills in our throats and a fishlike tail wrapped up our backs. As we continue to grow, the second or 'reptilian' brain forms. The foetus now bears a striking resemblance to that taken from a reptilian egg. The third growth stage is the 'mammalian' brain, which is when we begin to look like any mammalian embryo, until the fourth stage, the 'neo-mammalian' brain comes along, and we take on the form of a specialized mammal, a human.

The first thing that should strike you about this nine-month development is that it mirrors almost exactly the story of evolution. We came from the sea, we adapted to the land, we developed beyond our original mammalian structure. Just as, in the womb, we appear to possess a kind of tail during the early stages, so in later life we still bear the physiological traces of a species which once carried a tail. In other words, just as we have changed over millions of years, so we change during the nine months of growth in the womb.

If such change is inherent within the human species, inherent within the cells which make up the blueprints of our bodies, then perhaps we may activate change on our own terms. Perhaps we may use hypnotherapy to encourage the unconscious mind to stimulate physical growth and physical change?

Certain types of reptiles still exist which, when chased by a predator, discard their tails. While the predator eats the tail, the reptile escapes and subsequently grows a new one. It has even been known for very young babies who have lost the tip of a finger or toe to grow a replacement. The possibility exists for us to develop that ability as adults. Remember, one of the lessons of evolution is that nothing which is of use in the battle for survival is ever discarded; having experienced the notion of growth, both within the womb and as children, perhaps we have retained the knowledge behind the experience? Some of my work would certainly seem to point that way ...

Dr Alastair Reid MRCS, LRCP, DObst, RCOG, a general practitioner, tells the story of how he recommended one of his patients to come to me for treatment:

> Tracey Kitto received severe injuries to her left foot, in the summer of 1979 when she was fourteen years old and had been riding pillion passenger on a motor-bike.
>
> The injury was a severe compound fracture of the left calcaneum (heel bone) with considerable loss of skin tissue and also a portion of the bone. She was initially treated in hospital in North Wales and then locally by orthopaedic and plastic surgeons, and at one stage there were serious considerations given to amputation.
>
> I had heard Mr Keeton talking about the ability of primitive organisms to regenerate, to replace their damaged or amputated tissues, and wondered if it would be possible to stimulate the

more primitive brain centres and facilitate repair of the damaged structures and possibly some regrowth of the missing bone.

I subsequently discussed this with Mr Keeton and Tracey's parents, and we felt that an attempt would be justifiable on the grounds that no harm could possibly come from it, and it could possibly be beneficial.

Tracey had two sessions with Mr Keeton and proved an excellent subject for hypnosis. She was also given a code word whilst under hypnosis and told that when I used this code word in the correct circumstances she would enter the hypnotic state, and I would be able to boost the stimulation of the regeneration centres in the unconscious mind.

This transference worked extremely well, and still does.

The hypnosis proved extremely valuable as a psychological aid to ease the frustrations and anxieties which Tracey was suffering, and the improvement which occurred in the condition of her heel was much greater than any of her medical advisers anticipated.

Eventual recovery has been so great that this girl is now completing her third year as a nurse and will shortly be taking her state registration finals.

I can offer no incontrovertible proof that the hypnosis did provide growth stimulus, but I am convinced in my own mind that it did affect the healing process.

Many people report a distinct improvement in their hearing when they are under hypnosis – this seems to be because their unconscious minds are watching over them, thus enhancing their listening strength. But I have also had experience of people's hearing being improved even when they were suffering from faulty hearing before.

Mary is a good example of this. She lives in London and came along to one of our regressions being held in Wembley. When her turn came to attempt regression, she said, 'You will have to speak a little louder, I am almost deaf.' She went on to explain: 'The specialist told me that the nerve endings are deteriorating and nothing can be done about it.' Before I put her under hypnosis, I gave her a few simple tests to determine the extent of her deafness. Then I asked her to tune a portable radio to the volume setting at which she could comfortably hear the programme, and note the position of the volume control.

Mary achieved hypnosis very easily, and I taught her the technique of self-help. When she was roused, she found that the sound from the radio was much too loud: it was absolutely blaring and impossible to stand for many minutes. Since she herself had set the volume, and had noted it, there was no denying that her hearing had improved. And it continued to improve over the next few months until it was once again near perfect, which was confirmed by the specialist at the audiology clinic she had been attending. Whether or not Mary actually repaired the nerve endings in her ears we cannot say for sure. What cannot be disputed is her astonishing recovery.

Susan, who suffered from glaucoma, has had a similar success:

> Since I wrote to you, in May 1986, I have further good news. I had to wait until October before I had another visit to consult my specialist in London to ascertain whether or not I should require further surgery, this time on my right eye. As he was not too optimistic at my last consultation with him, I was of the opinion that surgery would be necessary. However, much to my delight, I was told that the pressure in both eyes was lower than before, and that my progress was amazing. Medication – that is, drops in my eyes – may be reduced in future. He says there seems no reason why my eyesight should not remain stable. Needless to say, you have and still do play a large part in having helped me in this very happy situation with my eyes. I practise many times during the day my relaxation exercises, which no doubt have been of tremendous value to me. I am convinced you gave me the help I so needed to fight my eye disorder.

Some of the success I have had in helping people improve their hearing almost certainly stems from the access they have been given to the greater powers of the unconscious. David, a fireman, began to notice some hearing loss and was told by both his doctor and an audiologist that nothing could be done to prevent the onset of total deafness. He was advised to consider the use of a hearing-aid. Naturally he was distraught, especially since in the fire service good hearing is essential.

After one treatment, I applied a test which I normally use with cases of bad hearing. I sent him down to the other end of the room – about 20 feet – and told him I was going to drop a pin onto a piece of paper. I asked him to turn around every time he heard the pin drop, and I varied the height of the drop from about six to about two inches. Every single time, David turned around the moment the pin hit the paper.

This kind of treatment, which we call hypnotherapy, really works by getting to the control centre of the whole body, the unconscious. Every body is made up of cells, and every cell is capable of the same function, since all cells duplicate the genetic information passed on by our parents. But for a body to be healthy, each cell must be instructed to perform only those functions for which it is needed. If a cell did not have such instructions and was allowed to produce any kind of tissue it liked, there could be no such thing as a stable species of human; mutation and deformation would be the norm. But the controlling unconscious acts as the guide and lays down the blueprint for cellular behaviour. In hypnotherapy, what we are interested in is encouraging the unconscious to correct the faulty instructions which are causing problems somewhere in the body.

We have already come across Liz Howard, the geneticist and novelist who has regressed to Elizabeth Fytton of Gawsworth Hall. In fact, she first came to my sessions because of her interest in regression, not from any desire for therapy. But routine questioning soon established that she had suffered from stomach ulcers for many years; she was on a strict diet, was allowed no alcohol and constantly used chemical pain-killers. I told her that her ulcers would soon disappear and that she would be able to give up her strict dietary regime. Naturally she laughed and told me that it was impossible; she had suffered for years, and no magic was going to take away that suffering overnight.

Within a few weeks, she had dispensed with the pain-killers, was able to drink alcohol and was off the strict diet.

> I gave it a year to see if the ulcers returned; they haven't. Now I must believe it.
>
> My life has been irreversibly changed by hypnosis. And not only, as people tend to assume, by the fascination of regression. True, regression was the basis for the historical novels for which I have since become famous, but it is the therapeutic side of your work which has been most significant. After a lifetime of misery brought on by over-production of stomach acid and a perforated duodenal ulcer, I am now able to relax completely. Hypnosis, as a method for instilling confidence and reducing underlying tension, is nothing short of miraculous, and I have to say that without your expertise a full-time occupation plus the publication of three novels within one year would have been impossible for me to achieve. Indeed, I should never have had the temerity to attempt to write, had you not insisted that nothing was beyond my capabilities. Despite working a regular fourteen-hour day, life is less frantic, less distressing and far more enjoyable.
>
> It is a great pity that embarrassing stage acts and the more frightening aspects of hypnosis – regression, for example – deter people from exploring the possibilities of hypnotic therapy in stress-related illnesses. In my own case it has not only relieved pain but removed the underlying cause of that pain by providing a new depth of self-awareness and greater powers of self-control. Hypnosis has given a new meaning to 'mind over matter', and the benefits are beyond price.

And another person who featured earlier in the book, Ann Dowling, has profited in health from her contact with hypnosis. In January 1978 she was admitted to hospital for the surgical removal of gallstones. After the operation, X-rays showed that she had developed several ulcers on the bowel. She asked me for help to get rid of them. A week later, when she returned to the hospital for further tests, she was told that the X-rays showed no trace of the ulcers; they had mysteriously disappeared.

Now, 'cures' like this inevitably take on an almost miraculous air, and those who do not understand the theory behind hypnotherapy often attempt to cast it in a somewhat lurid colour. They associate it with old wives' tales, such as the Derbyshire 'cure' for warts: you go down to the larder on the night of the full moon and steal a small piece of meat, then rub it on the wart. Having done that, you go outside and bury the meat, and as the moon wanes, so the wart goes. It may sound silly, but sometimes these 'cures' have been known to work, and we might conclude that, whatever one believes in, as long as one believes it strongly enough, a miracle will occur.

There is some sense to the argument, but if we are going to place our faith in the sense of our conviction, we might as well understand what it is we are trying to do. We are trying to activate the healing powers of the unconscious, so *that* is what we should believe in, not some old wives' tale. And by learning how to use the body's own immune systems, we can strip away all the superstitious nonsense and concentrate on regaining the powers that are latent within all of us. Leigh Richardson is a very courageous example of that idea; if only we all had his determination ...

The trouble for Leigh, a young man of eighteen, began with a swollen testicle. After a week's pain and silence, he confided in his mother, who made an appointment for him to see a consultant. He was advised to enter hospital for what he at first believed would be a minor operation. However, routine blood and urine tests showed that all was not as it should be. Despite the fact that he was suffering from severe stomach pains and sickness, he had no idea that all his symptoms were connected.

The entry in his mother Nancy's diary on 18 January 1985 says it all: 'Today Leigh was told he has cancer, and that it has spread to his stomach. I can't say how much I admire him and love him for his strength and his easy acceptance. He said he expected it and, in his usual casual way, went about his everyday life with a lovely sense of humour.'

Leigh's own diary entries are a lesson in stoicism. Never once does he complain of pain or discomfort but, like so many cancer victims, he expresses embarrassment at his loss of hair, which is one of the side-effects of the powerful drugs used to treat his condition. Violent and prolonged vomiting attacks also plagued him until he became so weak that he was a virtual shadow of his former self.

For a while, Leigh went into remission:

> The doctor said my scan was clear, but there was some swelling in the lymph glands – which meant more tests and more treatment. This time the drugs made my skin turn pale green and my urine dark blue.
>
> More tests, more X-rays, and more bad news. They told me that some of the cells were malignant. What could I do but make the best of it? Back into hospital I went on 18 February. I was surprised to find that many of the other patients were young, like myself.

Once more the chemotherapy (drugs cocktail) made him violently ill, but when the initial treatment was over, he begged to be allowed home to spend some time with a friend who was about to join the army. The two young men had a wonderful day out, but that evening his illness struck Leigh again like a ton of bricks. Feeling thoroughly wretched, he did not know what the future held for him – if indeed he had any future. He battled on bravely against the disease, but nothing seemed to help much. Then a friend of his mother's discovered an old newspaper cutting about my work in helping to treat cancer.

> My mum gave me the cutting and I read about the hypnotist who was successfully treating people suffering from arthritis and cancer by sending their memories back to the first cell that produced them.
>
> Quite honestly, I wasn't all that interested. I just read it to please my mum, then gave it back to her, thinking no more of it.
>
> A few days later, when my mum asked if I would like to see

this man, I said, 'Not really.' I didn't think he'd be able to do anything for me, because it only worked on a few people, but she insisted, telling me I had nothing to lose. Eventually I gave in and said I would go. At least it would stop her nagging.

Leigh responded immediately to the hypnotic induction.

I felt a warm sensation inside my body as the fighting cells began to kill the cancerous cells. While under hypnosis, I was taught how to combat the vomiting caused by the chemotherapy and the discomfort from the injections. When I was brought out of hypnosis I felt fine, and I had a warm sensation everywhere. I knew the treatment was working.

Then he taught me how to use self-hypnosis to relieve my asthma. I thanked Mr Keeton for all he had done, and couldn't wait to get home to try it for myself – and particularly to be ready for when I went into hospital again.

When I went in the following Monday, I felt a lot more relaxed than before, and I was really confident now that it was all going to work. After visiting hour, I relaxed for half an hour, telling myself I was not going to be sick when I came out of self-hypnosis. Sure enough, I was only sick once that day, although previously the treatment I was receiving had always made me violently ill. I slept better than ever before. But I couldn't make myself eat or drink.

I had been warned by the other patients that the treatment got worse as it went on, but for me it got better. Without hypnosis I would still have been lying in bed, being sick all the time. Instead I found that I could eat and drink and began to feel good. Now I use it to cure headaches and all sorts of things. Just to relax properly for ten minutes makes such a difference.

In tests made the first week after chemotherapy, before I had any hypnotherapy, my tumour count – which should have been well down – was still up. A week after my first visit for self-hypnosis the tests showed the count had gone right down. These tests are usually made at three-week intervals. The third test showed my tumour count to be clear.

Leigh is back at work in Harrogate as a joiner and enjoying

life again. His mother writes: 'On 7 December 1984 our family doctor said that Leigh would probably not be here next Christmas. Well, it's next Christmas, and he's here fit and well. No mother can ask for a better Christmas present.'

The power of suggestion is such that a medical diagnosis which states you have only a short time to live could in fact be *persuading* you to die. It sounds like a wild assumption, but then voodoo masters have known for centuries how to tell someone to die. It takes courage to resist such a diagnosis, and Leigh has shown plenty of that. Perhaps his example will show others that there are other ways to deal with disease.

Over the many years I have been practising hypnotherapy, I have been presented with all kinds of problems. I would like to go over now just a few of those cases, where the unconscious mind has conquered often the most debilitating diseases. All these cases serve to illustrate the argument for the therapeutic value of hypnosis.

Lesley was nine years old when she first developed a particularly disfiguring form of cancer on her face. Doctors held out little hope for her, until her mother brought her to me. Although she was younger than most of my patients, she was a bright little girl and responded well to the hypnotic induction. With her mother's help and the co-operation of her family doctor, she started to use the technique of self-hypnosis as a matter of routine; soon it became as much a part of her day as cleaning her teeth and doing her homework.

A month after we met, Lesley's mother telephoned me to say that the doctors were astonished with the progress she was making. The cancer on her face was beginning to disappear, and her general health was improving dramatically.

By the age of fourteen, Lesley had completely recovered and tests showed that there wasn't a single cancer cell left in her body. Now, at the age of eighteen, she has a full and healthy life ahead of her.

Her real name is not Lesley. As her recovery has been so complete, she is trying to put her brush with death behind her and prefers to remain anonymous. She, her parents and her doctor know her identity and her history; to others in her growing social circle, it is quite irrelevant.

A headmistress and a housewife came to me with serious, probably fatal, illnesses and completely recovered through regressive hypnosis. Their cases demonstrated another facet of this kind of treatment: when all other treatments have failed, patients are usually more than willing to give me their full co-operation and trust, which is precisely what hypnosis is based on.

David Stevenson, senior lecturer in international community health at the Liverpool School of Tropical Medicine, summed up his reaction to these cures: 'Somehow, Joe Keeton reaches down to the body's immune system. There is no doubt that his methods do work on some people.'

Cindy Crangle was a twenty-five-year-old artist I met during a visit to the north-west coast of America. For many years she had been restricted in her profession by eczema on her hands, for her skin could not tolerate contact with the many solvents and paints she had to use; sometimes even dipping her hands in water caused her great pain. The first time she ever experienced the malady was at the age of three, and at first it was very mild, appearing only when she was upset. But as the years went by, it increased in severity and frequency, and in her last year at college she had to abandon many classes and take alternative courses. Doctors gave her cortisone creams for local application, and relaxant barbiturates which left her feeling drugged. A naturopath relieved her most extreme symptons of itching and bleeding, but this cure was only temporary. Eventually she had to give up her job as a graphic artist and silk screen printer, while even enamelling was closed to her, because her hands could not tolerate the many acids and solvents used in the process. As she had tried so many cures by this stage, without any real change in her condition, she was surprised to find she was a good subject for hypnosis.

A year after I treated her, Cindy wrote: 'You will be delighted to know that my eczema cleared up completely after your treatment. My hands now tolerate all kinds of materials and solvents without any trouble at all. You can't know how much this means to me.' In fact, Cindy has now resumed her work on printing, enamelling and painting, and the problem has never come back.

Derek Whale, author and specialist writer on the *Liverpool Post and Echo*, describes his experience of hypnotherapy:

> I suffered the nagging pain of a duodenal ulcer for some twenty years and was never without a pocket full of antacid tablets. Although in the early years the ulcer once bled, I had no operation for this, and it continued to erupt occasionally – generally at times of stress or perhaps heavy physical work, like digging the garden.
>
> So, the day that I looked in on Joe Keeton to exchange a friendly word or two, I was not surprised to hear him ask if I was in pain. He had probably read it in my face.
>
> 'Have you got a pain about here?' he asked, indicating his hip. I said no, but that I had one in my stomach, and then briefly explained about my long-standing condition.
>
> Joe said, 'You won't get that pain again, and the ulcers will go.'
>
> I laughed. I knew that Joe, even in those early days before he became famous for his 'miracle' cures, was a sincere and genuine man who undoubtedly had the gift of occasional foresight and some healing prowess through hypnosis. But cure my ulcer without medication or surgery?
>
> 'All right, Joe, we'll see,' I replied. 'I'll give your forecast the acid test of time. If I have had no more attacks within, say, the next six months, I'll believe you.'
>
> That little incident took place ten years ago. I have had no ulcer pains at all since then.

Cliff Pattinson, whom we met in Chapter 4, has made use of a skill I try to teach people when I instruct them in self-hypnosis:

> I have found, at least to my satisfaction, that it is possible to arrest bleeding by hypnotherapy.
>
> The nature of my job is such that I occasionally knock little

bits and pieces off my hands and fingers; when this happens, I instruct my unconscious mind that when I count to four the bleeding will stop. It is successful every time.

I had been a regular blood donor for many years, having given a total of over 60 pints. I had had to use this new-found ability to stop bleeding a couple of times before my last visit to the clinic to give blood. On that occasion the nurses had the greatest difficulty in getting any blood out – they actually bruised my arm in their efforts.

The idea of reactivating their own, personal immune systems has an obvious appeal to doctors and nurses, many of whom now realize the benefits of these new abilities. Nurse Susan Suggett is one:

I have been using self-hypnosis since 1980, mainly as a means of coping with stress and controlling pain. I was aware that it was possible to control blood pressure and bleeding using the abilities of the unconscious mind, but it wasn't until about eighteen months ago that I had cause to try it.

I cut my finger whilst preparing vegetables, the type of cut that bleeds persistently. I sat down, closed my eyes and said, 'When I count to five, this bleeding will stop.' Sure enough, I opened my eyes after the number five, and there was a small clot of blood over the cut. It never bled again, and in fact healed much more quickly than is usual.

As a nurse I can see the advantage of being able to control bleeding in this way. Blood loss is a serious complication in many situations. The possibilities are quite obviously endless.

Mrs Morley-Kirk found an even more remarkable way to use her own immune system:

In February 1984 I suffered a cerebral haemorrhage and was admitted to the Queen's Medical Centre, Nottingham, and then to the neurosurgical unit at Derby Royal Infirmary. On admittance the doctors could not understand why I did not pass out with the pain, and also that I did not have to be held down when having a lumbar puncture. The surgeon was also surprised that he did not have to operate, as the haemorrhage healed itself.

My husband explained to them that I had been taught how to activate all my immune systems to make my body heal itself in the best possible way. My husband and I consider ourselves extremely fortunate to have met Joe Keeton, to be shown the wonderful power we have within ourselves and how to make use of it.

Multiple sclerosis, usually referred to as MS, is a degenerative disease of the central nervous system. When the sheathing with which our nerves are covered dies, the dead flakes enter the blood stream. We immediately start producing an antibody to remove the flakes, and in healthy people this production stops when no more flakes are found. With MS sufferers, the production continues after all the dead sheathing has gone, and the antibodies begin to attack the live sheathing on the nerves instead. They are literally eating their own nervous system. With cases of rheumatism, we try to stimulate the production of lubricant for the joints; with MS, we have to stop the over-production of this antibody.

Mrs Gill had MS. She walked only with great difficulty, and all feeling had gone from her finger tips. She came to me for treatment and soon learned the technique of self-hypnosis, which she put to good use. During their next holiday, her husband reported that she had walked them both into the ground. Mrs Gill's doctor told her to continue using the new technique, as it seemed more effective than anything he could offer.

That was in 1983. When I telephoned Mrs Gill for permission to use her name in this book, she agreed but said: 'I have had a marvellous two years, nobody could keep up with me. But it seems to be coming back and I am having some difficulty again in walking.'

It occurred to me that she might have been under renewed stress, and when I voiced that opinion she confirmed that she and her husband had had some serious problems recently. Once again, it seems that a very serious complaint can be induced by stress, and only the removal of that stress can make way for the removal of the complaint. It is important to continue with self-hypnosis methods, since without them the healing process can falter.

Asthma, hay fever and allergies respond readily to hypnosis. They all seem to be stress-related, and once the sufferer's own immune systems are functioning, they all disappear. One woman who came to me for treatment for arthritis happened to mention that she was allergic to gas fires, both portable and fixed. Before rousing her from hypnosis at the end of the therapy session, I placed a portable gas fire beside her. It stayed there for ten minutes, and no effect was noticed on her at all; indeed, she was happy to sit and chat without taking any notice of the fire. Her husband confirmed that previously this would have brought on a prolonged bout of sneezing and coughing.

The last case we shall consider in this chapter leads us on to the subject of the next. It involves the treatment of a malady by going back to the unconscious activity causing it, but it also serves to demonstrate how we may use hypnosis to analyse a psychological disorder. Such disorders, as we will see, can be manifested in behaviour; they can also, as with Diane, have physical symptoms.

Diane, a thirty-six-year-old woman from North Wales, had suffered from psoriasis since childhood. From the age of seven, blotchy patches had appeared all over her body, and no matter what coal-tar cream, oil, sunray lamps or herbs were applied, she only ever gained a temporary relief; under stress, the condition became even worse. It is sometimes not realized how debilitating such a disease can be, but in the summer Diane could never sunbathe or wear a swimsuit, and in her fashion style she was restricted to high necklines and long sleeves.

Her first visit to me was in October 1979, when she easily learned how to hypnotize herself and remove her stress through relaxation. Almost immediately, the blotches began to subside, and by the time of her second visit the following week, the scaly patches on her skin had cleared, and she felt more relaxed than she had for a long time. Soon, her skin ceased to flake and be irritable.

Diane was of course delighted, and she continued to attend my sessions because of her growing interest in regression. She accepted that a complaint such as psoriasis could not be a purely physical disturbance, and agreed to regress over her own life under hypnosis in order to find out what might have upset her so much that she developed the problem. As I led her slowly back through her own memories, a pattern emerged, whereby each time her psoriasis had worsened, she had felt under greater stress than usual. When I attempted to send her back beyond the age of eight – we both knew that the psoriasis had begun when she was seven – she became very distressed. Her heart began to race and her breathing became heavy, as if she was running very fast; she was clearly recalling a traumatic moment. Finally, after a long struggle between her conscious and unconscious minds, the true story emerged.

She was out playing with friends in some derelict buildings one afternoon. Suddenly, a man seized her, and all her friends ran away, leaving her to struggle on her own. She managed to free herself and ran as fast as she could. Sitting in front of me at the session, she vividly recalled the terror she had felt, which she had suppressed for so many years. So great was her fear that during the run home she forced herself to wipe the incident from her mind, and by the time she reached home it was as though it had never happened. Her parents knew nothing of it. She herself had never known she had been attacked until she saw it once more, almost thirty years later.

But if her conscious mind had forgotten, her unconscious had not, and ever since that day it had done its best to make her appear unattractive – presumably, unattractive to men. It had done its job with terrible success, and poor Diane has suffered all these years from a memory which was too dreadful to face. At least now she is free from its hold.

6 Psychological Healing

The man who relives the life of a soldier in the Crimean War; the woman who knows of the life of a nineteenth-century street urchin; the man who never thought his arthritis could be cured; the woman who faced the prospect of being unable to walk: they all share one common characteristic – the insight into the workings of their unconscious minds which they have gained through hypnosis. In all the wonder which surrounds the cases we have discussed so far in this book, there is never a trace of trickery or a suspicion of deceit. Everything I have described happened, nothing has been added or taken away, and hundreds of people scattered around the country are ready and able to confirm that this is so.

And yet how *can* it all be true? I sympathize with the question, for whatever we conclude about the results of my therapy and regression sessions, we can never say that they are easy to comprehend. For we are dealing with the one great mystery which still defeats the finest scientific minds: what really happens inside the human brain? A century of psychology has not brought us much closer to understanding how the unconscious works, and a thousand probes have still not elicited a fraction of the secrets which lie there. So how can we accept something so shrouded in mystique, so beguiling?

The answer, as I hope this book has gone some way to showing, lies in ourselves. If we only persist, we will gradually piece together more and more of the jigsaw of the mind. The cases described in this chapter show how much we can achieve by going back to the unconscious motivations for human behaviour; at the same time, they indicate just how far we still have to travel before we reach the goal of true understanding.

Phobias and other psychological disorders are difficult and frustrating to explain to those who have not suffered them. A broken leg, an infection – disabilities like this seem *real*, they give us something tangible to centre our sympathy upon. But when an otherwise healthy and intelligent person tells us he is unable to leave his house because he suffers from agoraphobia, he is more than likely to receive a response along the lines of, 'It's all in your mind. Don't be so silly. Get it out of your head.' The sufferer can often see disbelief in the other person's eyes, which then reinforces his problem by adding to it feelings of guilt and inadequacy. In fact, the damage caused to people suffering from a phobia by the almost hostile incomprehension of others causes them almost as much pain as the original phobia itself. The first step towards recovery for them is always the acceptance that their problem is not of their own causing and is therefore not something for which they should feel guilty.

So how do psychological disorders come about? They originate, of course, in the unconscious mind, which is built around a complex network of safety circuits. If we burn a finger on a match, our unconscious snatches the finger away; if we enter into a situation fraught with danger, our unconscious promotes the production of adrenalin; if we lose concentration while doing something, our unconscious either lets us carry on with the task or warns us that something is about to go wrong with it. Throughout our lives, we operate on these safety circuits, most of which are either inherited or learned from parents and teachers at an early age. And life itself – that provides lessons which our unconscious minds are not slow to learn from.

As we saw much earlier in the book, the unconscious is constantly recording our experience: good, bad, mundane, everything is stored away in the computer we carry about with us every day. Most of this information is just stored away, perhaps to be recalled again at a later date as a quirk of memory; but it also combines to give us an 'outlook' on life by which we conclude from everything we have experienced how we should view the world and its inhabitants.

Problems in later life, which we know as psychological problems, occur when our unconscious either misinterprets an experience or builds a safety circuit around the lesson of some incident which it is inappropriate for it to do.

Let me explain. The unconscious, during our crucial formative childhood years, can easily misinterpret the words and actions of influential people such as parents and teachers. If a child is told, 'You have a bad memory,' it is quite possible for this to be accepted by the unconscious as an instruction, in which case the child *will* develop a bad memory. If the ticking-off had been re-worded to 'You must improve your memory,' the result could be quite different. Similarly a teacher can cause untold damage to a child by humiliating it in front of a class. I have seen the results of such punishment methods as they are manifested in adults, and it is enough to make me wish that teachers could think a little before mocking a child's failure to learn in front of its friends and classmates. There are simpler and more humane ways to teach a child to add up or to spell. And punishment, too, can create unstable unconscious patterns, particularly when it is meted out by parents at home unjustifiably, for children have a very clear sense of justice, and a smacking when the fault was not with them can implant reactive feelings of guilt and resentment.

The cases we are about to look at dispel all such notions as, 'Well, she'll get over it.' They *don't* get over it, no matter how trivial the incident, and we should be on our guard against causing unnecessary trauma.

The second way in which psychological disorders come about is when the unconscious tries to deal with a frightening or upsetting experience. What it does in such a situation is to write in a programme to prevent the conscious mind ever experiencing such a trauma again. And remember, this

experience probably occurred at an early age, when the things
that frightened us would have no effect at all on us now. So by
programming us to avoid a similar situation, our unconscious is
making us avoid something which scared us at the age of six or
ten. That may sound absurd, and in a way it is, but you should
have some idea by now of just how powerful the unconscious
mind is: if it wants to impose such conditions, it can easily
override any argument from the conscious mind. From then on,
if the unconscious sensed this situation approaching, it would
put into motion a reaction to make us avoid it. And every time
we neared such a situation, this programme would actually be
reinforced, causing the disorder to deepen as we grow older.

In medical terminology, the depression which can result from
this unconscious activity is called 'endogenous', meaning that it
comes from within. It differs from 'reactive' depression, which
occurs as a result of some tangible misfortune, such as the loss
of a loved one or a failure at work. The endogenous depressive
cannot consciously pinpoint the cause of his weeping, his
headaches and his moods, whereas the reactive depressive at
least knows why he is depressed, and knows that time will heal
the wound.

The quickest and most efficient way to combat endogenous
depression and other psychological disorders such as phobias is
to take the sufferer through the memories of his life to relive
once again the experience which resulted in the problem. All
memories are stored in the unconscious, and through hypnosis
we may open it up for inspection, feeling once more all the joys
and pains of the life we have lived. Having reached and
experienced the incident behind the problem, the patient can
reassess it in the light of his adult experience, and put it in its
proper perspective, stripping it of its power to hurt.

Sometimes the unconscious will wriggle and give substitute
stories that could be traumatic enough to have caused the
problem, since its one aim is to protect the conscious mind from
ever having to think about the real incident over again.

Sometimes I find that patients have several experiences causing this kind of unconscious reaction, and removing them is like peeling layers off an onion, with all the accompanying tears and anguish. But although the treatment can seem hard, it does result in a cure, and for many people that can mean changing their whole lives.

There is another way of treating psychological disorders, for those who would rather not experience the trauma of reliving those harrowing experiences. It is a much lengthier treatment, although in the long run just as effective in curing the patient, and it too works through hypnotic communication with the unconscious. Patients are taught to instruct the unconscious to remove the apprehension, fear or embarrassment every time the feelings begin to manifest themselves. Eventually, the unconscious learns that its safety circuit for this particular incident is no longer needed, and so it cancels the programme.

But the cases we are now going to look at are those where the patients have decided to undergo hypnosis to go back over the memories of their own lives. Sometimes the event in early childhood which caused them so much difficulty in later life turns out to be so trivial and silly that they cannot believe how they could have been so badly affected. Often the reliving of past experiences causes considerable anguish, but its cathartic effect is undeniable. It sets the patient free from a disorder he had no way of coping with himself.

Individual Cases
MRS J.B.
Mrs J.B. came to me with a phobia about birds. Throughout her life she had panicked if a bird, no matter how small, came anywhere near her. A canary could make her tremble with fear, a photo of a robin could induce feelings of nausea. And yet not only did she have to suffer from this phobia every day of her life, she also had to put up with the patronizing attitude of those who

could not understand how she felt. How *could* she be frightened
of a lovely little bird! She should stop being so silly, and learn to
love them instead. Mrs J.B. put up with all the taunts and
suffered from her phobia until the day it almost killed her. She
was driving along a motorway with her husband when a bird
swooped down very close to the windscreen of the car. She
immediately froze in fear, and if her husband had not been there
to grasp the wheel, she would have crashed.

Under hypnosis, the young woman regressed back through
her life to her eighth birthday, when she refused to remember
any more. Gradually, month by month, I took her back from her
eighth birthday, when suddenly her heart began to race, and she
started to panic. Then she screamed: 'Susan! Get it away from
me! Get it away from me!' The screaming continued for a few
minutes, and then she was calm. Roused from hypnosis, she told
us what had happened:

'I had very long hair when I was a child. I was walking down
the path from our house to go to school. My friend Susan was
standing near the gate waiting for me. At the bottom of the
garden, on each side of the gate, was a fairly high privet hedge.
As I opened the gate, a sparrow, or some other small bird, flew
from the hedge and got entangled in my hair. It took ages to free
it from my hair.'

A few months later Mrs J.B. sent a picture-postcard of a
beautiful bird. On the back she had written: 'I am writing this
card at a zoo ... in an aviary.'

JACQUIE E.
Jacquie E.'s phobia was not at all dangerous; it just embarrassed
her. She became agitated if anyone, including her husband,
hugged her, and if someone trapped her arms for more than a
few seconds she became hysterical. She had never understood
why she felt like this.

Jacquie came to my sessions because of her interest in
regression, but her attempts to go back to pre-birth memories
were blocked by some incident in her own unconscious memory.

If she wanted to go beyond, she would have to clear this unconscious block first. (This often happens when people first attempt to regress; it is the effects of the block, the nature of the psychological problem which it causes, which differs from person to person.) It seemed likely that this block would be related to her phobia about being hugged.

We went back year by year through Jacquie's memories, all the way back to her first birthday, of which she retained a full unconscious memory. Although unable to converse while regressed to such a young age, she gurgled and uttered the words 'Dada' and 'Mama'; on being awakened, she was able to tell us what she felt and saw. Since she had had no difficulty in remembering everything to the age of one, whatever was causing her block must have occurred between her birth and her first birthday. She accepted the logic of this and insisted on locating the root cause of the problem.

This time, under hypnosis, she was taken back month by month, and then week by week until, just after she was born, she began to turn very red in the face and choke. Quickly I roused her from hypnosis and returned her to the present, when she was able to tell us what had happened. Someone – the midwife, Jacquie imagined – had wrapped a sheet around her, trapping her arms to her body. Then she felt a tube being pushed down her throat. She concluded that she had been born choking and that the tube had been inserted to clear the air passage.

Once we had found the trauma, and once Jacquie had relived it, she was able to see her phobia for what it was. She has never become upset by being hugged again.

JOHN

John first came for treatment because of his love of dressing up in feminine clothes. He had no desire to be mistaken for a woman – the fact that he wore a moustache was evidence enough of this – but he could not understand why he should feel such a compulsive desire to wear women's clothing. He wanted to try hypnotherapy to discover the reason behind it.

His mental blocks, once he was hypnotized, began to peel away, layer after layer. No sooner had we dealt with one problem than another emerged earlier in his life. He seemed to have had a particularly traumatic childhood and, from what we could tell, his worst experiences centred around one teacher at school.

As a child, John had been slim, with dark curly hair and a delicate, finely modelled bone structure. He was one of those boys who finds no pleasure in sports, who gain all their satisfaction from their academic studies. His one passion was drama, and it seems he lived for the school's theatrical productions. The teacher in question – a woman – obviously thought there was something wrong with a boy who didn't enjoy outdoor sports. She was one of those teachers who thought that a healthy body meant a healthy mind, and she put what seems to have been considerable effort in trying to shame John into becoming a 'normal' boy. Sadly, she only succeeded in making his life a misery, exacerbating his difficulties by constantly provoking him in front of his classmates.

Once regressed to his schooldays, he said, in a childish voice: 'She picks on me every day ... Look at John, he can't kick a ball ... Look at John, he can't swim ... He's more like a girl than a boy.' The crowning insult came at a prize-giving ceremony, when she presented him with a girl's dressmaking book, in front of the entire school. The other pupils were not slow to follow their teacher's lead, and he soon became an object of bullying and taunting for the rest of his unhappy time there.

Most patients who come to me with psychological disorders are suffering from a single traumatic incident. John's case was unusual in that he was suffering from so many blocks, and he needed three therapy sessions before he began to feel better. Then, having learned the technique of self-hypnosis, he seemed to need no more help in coming to terms with his problem.

Three months later he was back. He had recently gone into a room where his brother was watching a television programme about transexuality, featuring a man who had been surgically transformed into a woman. A few minutes of casual viewing brought all John's old fears and problems flooding back, and he returned for therapy.

Since we had dealt with the traumas of his schooldays and his vicious teacher, the blocks remaining within him must have stemmed from an earlier period in his life. I took him back again, year by year, to his pre-school days. He produced perfect memories of himself as a toddler, gurgling and spluttering like a baby, unable now to respond by language to our questions. Suddenly, as we were coming closer and closer to the time of his birth, he began to produce infantile screams, an extraordinary noise to hear coming from the fully developed larynx of a grown man. The screams were followed by a subdued whimpering, the unmistakable sounds of a baby in pain.

'That was amazing,' he said on his return to the present. 'I could feel myself being held and could see the head and shoulders of a nurse, and in front of me I could see the top of a man's head as he leaned over me. It must have been my circumcision.' John's mother confirmed his description of the nurse, so it seems he was indeed reliving the moment of his circumcision.

Could John's unconscious have reacted to the pain and fear surrounding his circumcision by promoting feelings of femininity? Could it have reasoned that this horror could only happen to boys and that, if he pretended to be a girl, it would never happen to him again? Who knows? The fact is, having undergone this final regression, John has never again shown the slightest sign of transvestism and has at last come to terms with the unhappiness of his childhood.

SHEILA
Hypnotherapeutic treatment is often hindered by unconscious attempts to mask the real cause of a problem. This can occur particularly where strong feelings of guilt are concerned, and it is often useful to have a relative of the patient in attendance to assist in the tortuous process of unravelling clues and decoding messages. Knowing the right path to take during therapy is half the problem.

Sheila, like John, needed more than one session to come to terms with her problem. She suffered from distress and depression, even though as a kind and sensitive person she was always willing to do her best to help others. Her daughter mentioned that Sheila's distress always increased during the month of August, in the run-up to her birthday, after which it would slowly subside again.

We established that in early adulthood her brother had fallen seriously ill, reaching a critical point during August. Sheila had naturally been worried, and her brother's suffering began to take its toll on her own health. Her husband and parents, seeing the effect it was having on her, virtually forced her to go away for a holiday. There was nothing, in their view, that Sheila could do, and her distress might even have an adverse effect on her brother. But while she was away, her brother died, and she was overcome with feelings of guilt that she had not been at his side when he passed away.

It was that guilt which had stayed with her, punishing her every day far more cruelly than any judge or jury could. As each August approached, these feelings welled up inside her and burst out again in a new suffering of grief and guilt.

Under deep hypnosis, I asked Sheila to re-examine the evidence surrounding her brother's death. I asked her to consider whether there was anything she could have done to halt his decline, or whether the holiday she had taken had in any way hastened his end. When she assessed the situation properly in her mind, she realized that the punishment she was giving herself was unjustified. At last she has stopped feeling guilty, and her depression and distress are a thing of the past.

MRS A.

It was guilt which lay behind Mrs A.'s heightened distress. She came for treatment in the company of her sister, who was worried that she might be approaching a nervous breakdown. The story she told was sad, senseless and ultimately avoidable.

Five years earlier, Mrs A.'s doctor had prescribed

anti-depressants, tranquillizers and sedatives in response to her high stress level. Like so many people, she kept these pills in the bathroom cupboard. One night, after she had taken her prescribed dosage and was sleeping heavily – effectively, a drug-induced sleep – one of her children, just three years old, wandered into the bathroom. The child clambered onto the edge of the bath, reached up to the cabinet and removed the contents. In her tranquillized state, Mrs A. had forgotten to lock the cabinet. The child probably thought the bottles contained sweets, and emptied them out and ate every pill. Within hours, Mrs A.'s child was dead.

It is not hard to imagine the extent of the guilt felt by Mrs A. Firstly, she had left the key in the lock of the cabinet. Then she had been too drugged to hear her child moving about in the house, whereas without the pills she would certainly have woken to the slightest unusual sound. But it seemed her guilt was reaching its peak only now, as another of her children was reaching the age when the other had died.

Under hypnosis, I began to explain to her why her guilt was unjustified. The drugs which doctors prescribe to their patients to cope with stress and depression are debilitating chemicals. They act on the body's nervous system in just the same way as alcohol, except their effect is to subdue the patient rather than to excite her. Taking these pills is like a motorist disconnecting a plug from a car – you are running on less than full power. But it is not your fault; it is the fault of your doctor who condemns you to subservience to artificial drugs. If anyone should feel guilty about the death of Mrs A.'s child, it should be her doctor, for prescribing the drugs in the first place.

Once I taught her the correct way to deal with her stress, Mrs A. came to realize that she need not carry on blaming herself for the past. Naturally, she will never be able to forget it, but at least now she knows she leads the kind of life in which it could never happen again.

SHARON BAYLIS

Sharon, a TV actress based London, tells her own story:

I'd suffered from 'infantile eczema' for as long as I could remember; not disfiguringly so, but enough to be a nuisance and an embarrassment. My hands were often red and raw, especially in winter, and as a child I had to suffer the nightly routine of tar ointment, bandages on arms and legs, and cotton gloves to stop me scratching in my sleep. Washing up aggravated it, as did household dust, peeling potatoes, touching raw fish. These, I knew, were not the cause of my condition, merely a symptom.

Nerves, even first-night nerves, did not seem to cause it, so I supposed it was not 'psychosomatic', as I had believed that was the only kind of stress I suffered from.

I am generally happy, an easy-going person, with a long fuse; in fact, I never lost my temper with anyone, except my parents and lately my husband. I knew that with them I could be irrationally and unreasonably angry and would snap at them for no apparent reason. It was the one thing I really hated about myself, but I kept my tantrums for when I was alone, afraid that, if anyone saw me hurling pillows at the wall and howling, they would be appalled.

I first met Joe Keeton at a friend's house. I was a member of a group of people who had asked him down to give therapy for various ailments. A friend told me it was a possibility that he could remove my eczema.

He talked to me for a while about how I saw myself and my life, and then suddenly asked me, 'What happened in that cupboard?'

Now, I've known a lot of cupboards in my life, but I knew without a shadow of a doubt that he was talking about the toy cupboard under the stairs in the house I lived in as a small child. Why that cupboard should come into my mind I don't know, but it wasn't long before I did.

Joe Keeton kept on talking to me and I found myself beginning to feel relaxed in my body, and at the same time more alert in my mind; all my senses seemed heightened. As I listened to his voice saying, 'I am going to count to ten. On the number ten you will be back in time to that cupboard in your childhood,'

I felt the most overwhelming rage growing within me. Though still aware of the room I was in, the chair I was sitting in and the other people around me, at the same time I was a three-year-old child, and I was inside that toy cupboard. It was pitch dark, but I could see the line of light coming in under the door, and I was having a tantrum. Tears flooded out. I could hear myself shrieking and sobbing, just the way a small child in an uncontrollable rage sounds. My body was curled up in the chair, but my right foot was kicking out furiously. One part of my mind was that of a three-year-old child; the other was adult and thinking of my friend's coffee table that was in front of my chair that must have been in danger of being kicked over.

I realized, though how I don't know, that I'd been shut in there because of the tantrum. I acknowledged, too, that the punishment was deserved and that I was in the wrong – which only served to make me angrier.

Gradually the feeling subsided and I was once again myself, sitting in a room full of people, with a very tear-stained face and a feeling of immense foolishness.

As I tried to describe the experience, I realized how ashamed I had always been of my temper, because I knew that if it got out of control … what? I'd be shut away in the toy cupboard? Yet I had no conscious memory of that ever having happened. Nevertheless, fear of something had caused me to repress my anger to such an extent that even my closest friends had never seen it. Only my parents and my husband, whom I knew would still love me anyway, were aware of it, though even they had not seen the full extent of my anger.

I suddenly realized that there is nothing wrong with justifiable anger, or even temper, so long as it is not turned inwards to become destructive.

I later asked my parents if they could remember ever having shut me in the toy cupboard as a punishment. My mother looked blank, but my father shamefacedly said he did remember one such occasion. It was a Saturday afternoon, when I was quite tiny and he was looking after my brother (four years older) and me. A squabble broke out over a toy, and I had a tantrum, apparently not unusual when I was very little, and in desperation he shut me in the cupboard until I had calmed down.

He remembers standing outside the cupboard door, listening to my sobbing and shrieking, and the sound of frantic kicking at the door. It was a very trivial incident, but enough to affect me for the next twenty-seven years of my life.

I lose my temper now, not often, only when necessary, and the knowledge that I can lose it somehow means that it is rarely necessary to do so. And I haven't had the slightest trace of eczema since.

MRS J.A.

Sometimes, instead of blocking off all the events that cause a problem, the unconscious substitutes a memory which, although frightening, is more acceptable to the conscious than the truth.

Mrs J.A. had been under psychiatric help since shortly after her sixteenth birthday. She had told the psychiatrist a disturbing story. One night, she said, she was walking through town on the way home when two youths seized her and pushed her towards a nearby block of maisonettes. She screamed and struggled in her efforts to escape, but to no avail. The youths had almost forced her inside the entrance of the long block when a man came by. He was walking his dog and whistling a popular tune, and Mrs J.A. could even remember the tune. At the sight of the man, as she recalled them to the psychiatrist, the boys let her go.

Obviously this was a frightening experience, and it would have had some kind of effect on the girl. But for it to still be exerting such an effect that twenty years later Mrs J.A. was still taking tranquillizers, there must have been more to it than she had claimed.

It took several sessions of the very deepest form of hypnosis to extract the complete story from Mrs J.A. First, we discovered that there had not been two boys but four. Then we found out something worse – there had been no man out walking his dog.

Bravely Mrs J.A. insisted on reliving the experience, and we watched and heard as she struggled against the rape, screaming throughout. After it was over, she hammered on the doors of the nearby maisonettes, begging for help, but no one answered. A girl screaming in pain and terror as she was raped, then banging on doors asking for help – and still no one heard. Surely *someone* must have heard?

When she arrived home, just after eight o'clock, both her parents were out. She took a bath and went to bed. By the time she got up in the morning, her unconscious mind had erased the horror of the night before and had substituted it with the story she was to tell her parents, and later the psychiatrist. There was no deliberate conscious decision involved and, until she came to me for therapy, she had no idea that she had been raped. If any proof is needed of the power of the unconscious mind, there could be none better than Mrs J.A.'s story.

Today she remembers everything about that night, and she has adjusted to the truth of the past. She takes no tranquillizers any more.

MICHAEL BOTT

Even at the deepest levels of hypnosis, the unconscious still applies its own rules. If some trauma that is being re-experienced is considered too awful for the conscious mind to bear, the unconscious will bring itself out of hypnosis and stop the experiment. This kept happening to Michael Bott: just as it seemed he was getting close to the root of his problem, he came out of hypnosis. It took us many sessions before the truth was uncovered.

Michael is an actor, and if there is one thing an actor can do without, it is a speech impediment. Let him tell the rest …

Strangely enough, before I met Joe I was not aware I had any problem with my speech. I knew I had difficulty in expressing myself fully, but I thought that that was just 'me' and not a difficulty which could be cured by some form of therapy. A stutter or an impediment is an obvious affliction, but my problem was more subtle, so subtle in fact that no one had ever pointed it out to me until Joe surprised me by asking why I had difficulty in talking. Gradually the truth that I did have a difficulty dawned on me as I began to monitor my own speech, hearing how disjointed it was, often how unclear the sense was, and the way in which, in order to make myself understood, I would have to backtrack and make corrections, editing myself as if I were a typist going back over my script. The overall effect was not that I sounded stupid or nonsensical, but I lacked confidence and conviction in what I was saying.

Now, to someone in my profession, that is nothing short of disastrous; I had no difficulty when on stage or in front of the camera having learned the script, but in the competitive area of the interview or audition for the job it would be a very astute person who could see through my involuntary smokescreen and be sure that I was capable of expressing myself properly in a professional situation. Also directors and casting directors prefer to see a certain amount of confidence in the actors they are going to employ (as do any people looking at prospective employees – it makes them feel more comfortable), but my difficulty made sure that self-confidence was something I was not projecting.

At first I could only reason that the cause must be my perfectionism, a quality of mine Joe had already mentioned. It seemed that when speaking I was always interfering with my true flow of thought – the true expression of myself – by trying to imagine some 'correct' response to whatever was asked, or said, by other people, consequently falling between the two stools of pleasing my listeners and being truthful to myself. At its extreme, a perfectly simple question would leave me unable to answer, throwing me into an overwhelming yet silent panic which would take several minutes to subside.

How was it I had managed to accept for so many years something that was manifestly so damaging to myself?

It is a very simple matter to ask a person to relive their most dreadful experience, but it is very hard for the person concerned to allow it to happen. Even under hypnosis, in which many people mistakenly assume that the hypnotist is in control of the subject, it takes a great deal of courage to allow the unconscious mind to provide the moment which one is looking for and, more often than not, a deal of time exploring the false avenues as the conscious mind interferes, avoiding the event with a desperation proportional to the degree of trauma involved. But sometimes what was significant in the past viewed from the present seems inconsequential, even to the point of being comical – small events often resulting in devastating effects. So it was with me.

Having established that my 'block' was to do with being humiliated in front of people, at last I allowed myself to be drawn back to that moment. Hearing myself crying, 'I don't know, I don't know,' over and over in response to the question, 'What's the matter, Michael? What don't you know?', as my voice became more childlike and desperate, I was again overwhelmed with that very humiliation that I had spent most of my life trying to avoid. My eyes were closed and I was unaware that my fingers were working furiously as an infant's, desperately trying to count on his hand but lacking the co-ordination necessary to move them in an order that would give the numbers he was seeking. 'What are you counting, Michael?' I heard Joe ask, and an instant later, under the sound of my own voice screaming, 'I don't know, I don't know,' I heard in my head the question which had troubled me for probably twenty-five years:

'What is two plus three?'

A fleeting vision of the teacher's face passed before me and an awareness of a whole class of know-all infants around me. Everyone knew the answer but me. The question was simple, but my mind had become a conundrum of shame, guilt and failure. I never answered the question.

A simple sum resulted in a humiliation that, up to the present, had made me frightened of being 'wrong' in whatever I said – as if there was always some 'correct' answer, or response, to what other people had asked or said. I was terrified of not knowing the answer. I never spoke what I thought, rather what I imagined others wanted me to say, and that had been my problem.

I know now that my answering or not answering the question was really unimportant and, by the same token, that I need never fear what does or does not come out of my mouth.

Since I faced that awful situation again, my everyday speech has improved enormously, and even people who may not have noticed a problem with my speech in the past have remarked that they see a new poise and confidence in me. I suppose I could say that the difference in me is like the difference between a schoolboy who, when asked a question, has to look up the answer in the back of the book, only to find the pages missing – and the schoolboy who knows the answer, or at least has a bloody good guess!

I believe that our basic personalities are as immutable as our fingerprints. What happened to Michael in that classroom (and, as we discovered, later at the hands of his mercilessly taunting schoolmates) affected him so greatly because of the perfectionism embedded in his character. Another child might have sailed through such an ordeal, not caring that it could not add two and three together, but to Michael there could have been no greater humiliation.

RAY BRYANT

That someone who, in regression, has experienced the life of a Crimean soldier should be scared of spiders sounds ridiculous, but not so to Ray. His phobia is an excellent sample of how the unconscious can distort experience in its attempt to protect the conscious mind.

> For as far back as I could recall, I had had an utter abhorrence of spiders – without knowing why. It was not just a simple fear. The sight of even a quite small spider would make me feel ill, and the thought of one landing on me would send me into near panic.
>
> Of course, it was an embarrassing phobia for a six-foot-tall, apparently quite normal man, master of a household.
>
> It was all right when only my wife, Audrey, was present. She got to understand and she accepted that, if a spider did appear in the room, she would have to be the one to put it out. She knew that if any other living creature emerged – snake, lizard, beetle, wasp, wild dog or whatever – I would quite happily tackle it. Spiders, no. Definitely no.
>
> The real embarrassment arose when other people were in the house, friends or relations, perhaps, who could not so readily understand a spider phobia. Then if a spider appeared and they pointed it out, I had either to pretend to fail to see it, or fail to reach it before it scuttled into some inaccessible corner.
>
> It was a constant annoyance, but I thought it was the cross I would have to bear all through my life. I knew there were times when it would cause me not just embarrassment but actual physical suffering, like the time some unknown person apparently realized my fear and sent me a live spider in a box. I'll

never forget how sick I felt when I opened that parcel, and the poor creature ran out of captivity straight at my arm.

Then came the day I went to Joe Keeton out of an interest in hypnotic regression. I was interested in regressing to past lives, not getting rid of phobias. At that time I did not realize that phobias could be cured by hypnosis, nor did it occur to me that I would have to clear memory blocks such as those which caused phobias in order to regress fully.

When I did try to regress and found my memory blocked at around the age of seven, I could not understand what terrible thing it was in my childhood I was afraid to face. It took twelve consecutive sessions of persuading and bullying me through it before the story came out, the story I had not realized was there to be told.

Gradually the nightmare scene came through. I was standing on the stairs in the house in which I lived at the age of seven, and at the top of the stairs there was something so awful I could not bear to look at it. I knew its shape but my mind refused to recognize it or let me look.

Under deep hypnosis, I went through that agonizing scenario again and again before I convinced my subconscious that I really did want the answer. Crying and screaming like a seven-year-old before the eyes of all the others at the regression group, I finally allowed the whole picture to come out.

It was just after the war. The first six years of my life had comprised many nights of being awakened and hurried out to air-raid shelters. My father was a sailor and, because my mother wanted us to be with him as much as possible, she took us to places where he was stationed, such as Liverpool, Glasgow and Plymouth, all of which suffered heavy bombing raids. It had left me a nervous child, and for long after the war I suffered both nightmares and sleepwalking, sometimes both at once.

But it was on one particular night that my terrible memory block had formed. I had seen a Tarzan film in which people had been eaten by a six-feet-tall spider. That night I went sleepwalking again, down the stairs, and in my walking nightmare the giant spider reappeared at the top of the stairs. I screamed out. My mother was awakened and came running to me in a mild panic. But in my nightmare, it was not she who came hurrying down the stairs to grab me up but that huge, disgusting spider.

I was astonished when all that came out of the regression. I'd no conscious memory of any such thing happening to me. I must have blocked it out of my conscious immediately that spider got me in its jaws, but the horror of spiders had lived on.

And now? The sight of spiders no longer bothers me. I have even touched them, in particularly bold moments. Usually, however, I simply ignore their presence.

I wouldn't claim that I liked the things now. But then, after a nightmare like that, would you?

JENNIFER

From early childhood, Jennifer had to be very careful with knives – in fact she had to keep away from them, because even the sight of one would give her an urge to slash her own throat. When the family sat down to a meal, no knives were allowed on the table; meals out in restaurants were a particular problem and, unless the host was sympathetic, parties were impossible. She began to feel like a social outcast.

Under hypnosis she was able to go all the way back in her memories to the age of 5½ when she came to an abrupt halt. She curled herself up in the chair, feet tucked under her with her knuckles stuck into her mouth, and her eyes screwed shut. She was no longer a young woman; she was a terrified child. We could not get a word out of her, although she was obviously going through something very traumatic. When it seemed she had been in that state for some time, I gently brought her back to the present, telling her to retain full memories of what she had just experienced.

She told us that she was in her parents' home, watching a television programme on Jack the Ripper, or a story like that, and that the combination of terror and fascination was gluing her to the set. With her adult perspective, she could now see how she had developed such a dangerous phobia.

The following day we received a telephone call from her. She told us that, when she had got home the night before, she had taken every knife she could find in the house, put them in a large circle on the floor and then sat in the middle of the circle for over ten minutes. Her phobia was conquered.

MRS M.
Mrs M., a retired hospital matron, was a pillar of the community, conscientious and law-abiding. Her phobia, then, was all the more remarkable: she was terrified of policemen. Even if she was driving her car, the sight of a police van would disturb her so much that she had either to stop or to change direction.

Her unconscious block manifested itself under hypnosis between the ages of six and seven. She broke down in tears, but through her sobs she managed to tell us what was happening. She was in her bedroom, where her father had sent her after he had found out she had broken an ornament in their next-door neighbour's house. Her father told her that she was to stay in her room while he fetched a policeman to take her away. A few minutes later she heard slow, heavy footsteps coming up the stairs, becoming louder and more menacing with every step. As they approached the room, the child's terror reached fever point – as did the matron's, under hypnosis. 'God, I was terrified,' she said after the session – but at least she now knew where her irrational fear came from.

Her father's threat seems appalling to us now, although it was often used by parents a generation ago. With his dramatic performance, however, he managed to take it a little further than was usual, and in the process unwittingly brought about a serious phobia in his own daughter.

PAUL H.
Paul H. was eighteen when he first came to a session. He was fascinated by ghosts, spiritualism and other psychic phenomena and was convinced that when he was younger he had had a brush with death. What is more, he was sure that a ghost or guardian angel had saved his life.

Before I put him under hypnosis, Paul told us of his conscious memories of the event. He said he had been playing in a park near his home, where the council had erected an old telegraph pole fitted with swinging ropes, in an adventure playground. It seems they had not buried the pole deeply enough, for one day Paul and a friend watched with horror as it began to topple down towards them. It seemed to be heading straight for Paul, when he felt something push him to one side seconds before he estimated it should have hit him. Instead, the pole hit his friend and killed him.

Consciously, Paul insisted that the pole should have hit him and that, were it not for his guardian angel, it would have done so.

It took him several sessions before he could bear to face his friend's death again, but finally, in deep hypnosis, he relived the tragic incident. His voice was quivering with fear, and he was half sighing, half sobbing, 'I can't move, I can't move.' Then his tone changed to one of complete surprise, and he said, 'I have moved.' Terrified, he kept repeating his friend's name, looking down at the boy who lay dead at his feet. 'I'm floating,' he said, in an eerie voice. 'I'm floating away.'

'You are not floating away,' I told him.

'It's my fault … it should have been me.'

'It is not your fault, and you are not floating away. Has someone gone for an ambulance?'

'They've all gone … Now someone's come back … It's … It's … Someone's moved me … I've moved …'

'You're not paralysed. You can move and you are not paralysed and you are not floating away.'

'But the post … the post fell round me.' Then he began to shout. 'It's the rope on top … it swung round … It should have been me.'

'It should not have been you, Paul. None of this is your fault.'

'But the rope swung it round past me … It missed me, and it hit him.'

And so, after all this time, he finally learned the truth: it was no ghost which had saved him but a safety rope which had swung the pole past him. With this knowledge, Paul was able to accept that he should feel no guilt, that there was nothing he could have done to save his friend's life. He no longer felt he had committed a crime by surviving when his friend had died.

FURTHER CASES

I do not have room in this short book to go over all the cases of psychological disorder I have dealt with in my years as a hypnotherapist. They cover an incredible spectrum of complaints, from minor irritations to terrible debilitating diseases, but, as I hope I have shown, they all share the same pattern of unconscious repression which may be released only through true hypnosis. Perhaps these last few cases will help show how phobias both share this common characteristic and display their own unique peculiarities.

Peter H. had been suffering from depression for years, had been taking prescribed medication, and all because of his fear of the Atomic Bomb. He revealed this under hypnosis, saying that it was the fear of a slow death from radiation which was the root cause of his depression. When it was suggested to him, he agreed that, if he moved into the middle of the city, he would be in the exact spot where the bomb would fall, and so would die immediately. Crazy it may be, but you have to admit it has a certain logic to it! Peter moved straight away into a house in the middle of town, secure in the knowledge that, if a nuclear war ever breaks out, he will die straight away. His depression has disappeared.

Mrs W., a twenty-nine-year-old mother of four, had a horror of newspapers, television news and anything to do with current affairs. Her phobia became so bad that she could not even walk past a newsagent without feeling sick. Then she began to worry that the tablets she was taking might be damaging her system.

Under hypnosis, she revealed that she had lived on an RAF station in West Germany when she was first married. She could remember the sirens going off on a practice nuclear alert, and once more she felt helpless in the face of her situation. For, as she realized, it wasn't really the idea of war which had upset her, it was the idea that she was still only twenty, already pregnant with her second child, and was 'missing out on life'. Her unconscious used the idea of war and nuclear weapons to disguise her own disappointment that life should have taken the course it had for her. Ten years on, having faced those feelings, she was able to rationalize them, and at the end of the session she proved she had overcome her phobia by reading a newspaper without a trace of fear.

Wendy was a student teacher, in her early twenties and working in her chosen career, who suffered from the occasional bout of inexplicable depression. Under hypnosis she remembered that at nursery school a teacher had punished her for kicking over a classmate's building bricks. Instead of punishing her in a reasonable way, the teacher had made her sit in a baby's high chair in front of the whole class – again, a form of ritual humiliation rather than any constructive form of punishment. Wendy's distress when she called the incident back to mind after so many years was an indication of how deeply it had been embedded in her unconscious. Interestingly, the incident also helped convince both Wendy and her colleagues about the dangers of shaming young children in front of their peers; they all vowed never to do it once they completed their teacher training.

Doreen suffered from unconscious guilt, prompted by her strict adherence to her religious beliefs. She was stuck in an unhappy marriage which she believed she could not leave, both because she felt this would break her marriage vows and because she had four children. The very thought of leaving her husband, however unhappy she might have been, put her into a state of anxiety neurosis. So obsessive was this guilt that she even failed to realize that all four children were receiving medication for their nerves, as a direct result of the tension in the house. In a light state of hypnosis, I advised her to go and have a word with one of the clergy at the church she attended, which she did, within the week. To her surprise, she was told that a divorce was possible, even advisable – and her tension and feelings of guilt vanished.

Barbara proved one of the most difficult cases I have had to solve, mainly because the punishment she had inflicted upon herself was so severe. She had suffered from tension and depression for over thirty years, and by the time she came to me she was consumed by unhappiness. She was a nurse, living in the north of England, and she and her husband were not wealthy. Her mother and sister lived in London, and she could not afford the fare to travel down and visit them very often. When her mother fell ill and was admitted to hospital, Barbara began to feel bad about not being with her; when her mother then died of a sudden stroke, she was inconsolable. Her grief and guilt were later compounded by her sister's censure, and for the next thirty years she punished herself for a crime she hadn't committed.

Having faced her mother's death once more, this time under hypnosis, we showed Barbara the truth of the matter: how she had been unable to afford to travel down to see her mother, how she had responsibilities at the time to look after her own children, how the sister who later accused her of not caring lived very close to her mother's hospital, and so could visit without any difficulty. It took a long time, but finally she believed us, and finally she stopped hurting herself.

The only thing wrong with Danielle, a beautiful young woman in good health, was that she could not stand her own sister. She had no idea from where the enmity arose towards her younger sister, until we took her back to the age of 2½, when her sister was born:

'Where are you, Danielle?'
'In a room.'
'Where?'
'At home.'
'Are you all right?'
'Ye...s.'

'What's the matter?'

'My mummy's got a new baby in her arms.'

'That's nice.'

'No, it isn't. Nobody looks at me any more.'

'That's all right. It's just because she's new. You're very pretty. They will look at you.'

'No, they won't … and my mummy has to feed it.'

'Doesn't your mummy feed you?'

'Oh yes, but it's not the same. She has the baby on her knee to feed it.'

'Do you want her to feed you the same way?'

'With that stuff? Yuk!'

'Well, then …'

'Nobody looks at me any more. They all want to see the baby.'

'Ah, but just think about when it gets older. You will be able to play with it, won't you?'

'Ye...s.'

'You will always be able to tell the baby what to do. She will always be younger than you.'

'Always?'

'Yes, always.'

'She'll never be my age?'

'No, never.'

'Ohhh!'

Sometimes, to resolve a conflict, it is necessary to use just a touch of cleverness. When recalled from hypnosis, Danielle remembered this exchange and realized she had been suffering from a childhood grudge for the whole of her life. Her unconscious had dictated the terms for long enough – and her sister certainly deserved a break!

Psychological healing and past-life regression

Sometimes I take a patient all the way back through his or her life and still find no trace of the cause of the trauma from which they are suffering. So long as they agree, I then take them back to pre-birth memories, to try to find the cause there. The results of this kind of treatment are as satisfying to the patient as they are when the trauma is found at some point in the patient's own lifetime, but they are all the more interesting for the light they cast on the theories discussed in Chapter 4 of hypnotic regression.

Before I describe some of these cases, I should stress something which I mentioned earlier. No one is forced, under hypnosis, to say anything they do not wish to say. No patient has to answer a question if he or she doesn't want to, and no one has to explain the cause of a trauma if they prefer to keep it to themselves. But they do have to relive it, if they are to rid themselves of its influence.

Pauline had been frightened of heights for all of her twenty years, but nothing in the memories of her own life gave any reason for such a phobia. Once I had told her to search for any other memories in her unconscious mind, however, her breathing became very agitated and her heartbeat began to race. She was obviously under great stress, and it took her three sessions before she could face the incident she was reliving. This is what she told us about it:

> I said I was the fifteen-year-old son of a London gentleman who worked in a bank. My name was John Roberts. I had been to public school, and we lived in a large house overlooking Regent's Park.
>
> It was towards the end of the last century. I was standing on the third-floor balcony of the house watching a parade pass by in the street below. I described a gold coach and mounted soldiers in their colourful uniforms.
>
> Next I was lying on the ground looking up at a rider whose horse was rearing in terror. I saw the horse's hooves coming down towards my head. Then there was nothing.

Here is Pauline's mother's report of the regression: 'Pauline is a Scouse, with a fairly strong Liverpool accent, and I was amazed to hear her voice and accent change to a refined accent, just like a gentleman's son. An interesting thing is that she has always been a very intelligent child. She could read and write before she went to school.'

A few days after the treatment, a newspaper photographer took her up to the roof of a high building in Liverpool, and took a picture of her leaning over the edge. Reliving the experience of the past-life regression had obviously cleared her phobia about heights; but was the regression true?

Since the event had sounded like the Golden Jubilee procession of Queen Victoria, we went to the files of the *Liverpool Echo* and found many pages reporting the parade. Almost at the end of the report were two lines: 'Several people fell from points of vantage.' We got no further in our research, but the most important fact remains that Pauline has lost her fear.

Jack Pleasant, a feature writer for *Weekend* magazine, tells the story of Carol Masters:

> When I attended one of Joe Keeton's sessions for the first time, as a sceptical journalist, I was introduced to pretty twenty-three-year-old Carol Masters, who had volunteered for regression.
>
> I asked her if she was married and she told me that she was, but that she had no children and didn't want to have any until she was at least twenty-six. Curiously, she said she had been maintaining this since she was a girl, though she did not know the reason why, only that she 'just didn't want to'.
>
> Under Joe Keeton's hypnosis, Carol quickly regressed, apparently to become Catherine Jeffries, a farrier's wife living in the then village of Woking, Surrey, towards the end of the last century. She spoke interestingly about life in those days until, startlingly, she began to go through the pangs of childbirth.
>
> The year was 1898. Catherine Jeffries was twenty-five.
>
> And the childbirth proved fatal, both she and the baby obviously dying. Joe Keeton quickly brought Carol out of hypnosis.
>
> It seemed a remarkable coincidence that a young woman, who in this life had long maintained irrationally that she did not want babies until she was past twenty-five, had apparently died having one at that age in a previous life.

Is it possible that the death of poor Catherine Jeffries nearly a hundred years ago was somehow linked to Carol Masters' present-day phobia?

I find the idea very tempting to accept, especially as I followed up Catherine Jeffries' story, visiting Old Woking, as it is now, close to the more recently built part of the town. The mill on the River Wey that Carol described under hypnosis had existed until it burned down thirteen years ago. The church does have a tower, and not a spire, as she insisted.

A family named Martin did own a local shop in the 1890s, from whom she said she bought cloth to make her own clothes.

Carol Masters (not her real name, by the way) was living in Liverpool when I met her in 1977 and had never visited Woking in her life. Joe Keeton has lost contact with her now.

It would be interesting to know if she did eventually have a baby. And if so, did she leave it until she was past the age of twenty-five, the age when Catherine Jeffries died in childbirth?

A young married woman in Birmingham who came to one of my regression groups revealed that she had always been obsessed with Oxfam and any charity to do with deprived children. It was not just a case of occasionally giving away some money: even as a child she had constantly gone out of her way to help children in need. At her first regression session she went back to the English Civil War and began to scream that she was about to be dragged away to be hanged for the murder of her two children. After several sessions, we discovered that her husband had gone to serve in the Roundhead army and that she had been left to fend for herself and the two babies. Gradually her living conditions worsened, until she and the children were actually starving, and in desperation she smothered them rather than see them starve to death. Obviously a case like this is virtually impossible to corroborate but, true or false, it is a remarkable explanation for a grown woman's inexplicable obsession.

I have come across other cases of apparent past-life memories influencing the unconscious attitudes of the present: the committed hunt-saboteur who regressed to a kitchenmaid who had been savaged to death by her master's hounds; the backache sufferer who regressed to a character from the previous century whose fall from a balcony had caused severe back injuries; the woman with perpetually cold fingers, who regressed to a farm boy whose fingers were caught in a bailing machine. All three overcame their difficulties once they had experienced their regressions, but who can say whether these experiences were 'real' or not? Perhaps one of the lessons of this book is that we should not be so sure about what we consider the word 'real' to mean.

7 Conclusion

Just occasionally I have been able to help people change the way they use their minds so much that they have developed the ability of total recall. I am indebted to the editor of the *Liverpool Echo* for granting permission to quote verbatim from Chris Barrow's report in that paper of Linda Neville-Jackson's story:

Thanks to hypnosis, Linda Neville-Jackson has a photographic memory. And that means that, instead of having to rummage through filing cabinets for an important document her boss needs urgently, Linda just closes her eyes and 'sees' it.

This ability of instant recall puts her in a class of her own, and she never fails to amaze her boss, who is chief executive of the Land & Marine Construction Company at Ellesmere Port.

'In fact,' chuckled Linda, 'I don't think he knows how I do it. I have told him that I have been undergoing regression therapy with a hypnotist, but I am not sure that he realizes that a photographic memory is a spin-off.'

Linda decided to volunteer for the sessions with hypnosis expert Joe Keeton after she heard him appealing for volunteers on a television show.

'I was interested by the claims he made and decided to act as a guinea pig,' added Linda. But she has had to work on her new-found talent. 'They say practice makes perfect ... and it seems to be the case with me, though it doesn't work too well outside the office,' she said.

As all secretaries know, the boss is always losing something and needs a good personal assistant around him – if only to join in the paper chase.

'Before taking a course in hypnosis I had been through the hunting high and low bit with previous bosses,' said Linda. 'Now I don't have the problem. When something has been put down – and sometimes it is in one of those safe places that you never look until everything else has failed – my mind takes a picture of it. When, sometime later, my boss asks for it, I know exactly where to go to find it.'

A light-hearted example maybe, but true enough and significant enough to serve as a lesson.

What I hope to have shown in this book is that we are still a long way from comprehending the human mind. As someone once said, the problem with understanding the brain is that we have only a brain with which to understand it. Every day we let the powers contained within our minds lie fallow, while our bodies suffer from disease and our lives are damaged by the stress of everyday life. Every day our unconscious minds act, unknown to our conscious minds, to help us survive. Every day we grow further and further from what we might be.

The examples quoted in the book show just how much is waiting to be discovered within the unconscious. The memories of past lives, the blueprints for the powers of healing, the safety mechanisms that protect us – they are all part of this thing we call the unconscious. Once, when we were hunters and depended on our natural skills for survival, we were at one with our unconscious minds. They let us sleep at the drop of a hat, wake refreshed when we were ready and become alert the moment any danger presented itself. We depended on our unconscious minds to heal us when we were sick, to see us through hardship and to protect us from weakness and fatigue. Then, over the centuries, we became more and more sophisticated, relying increasingly on our conscious abilities to change the environment in which we lived, rather than allowing our unconscious minds to adapt to those circumstances. Of course, we have profited from our ability to change the world. But we have profited at the expense of the harmony which once existed within our minds. Where once they co-existed, the conscious and the unconscious now appear to struggle. We suffer from phobias, we are highly strung, we fight to make our mark on the world rather than just to live. We have grown more and more dependent on our conscious minds and have systematically neglected the huge capacity of the unconscious.

The man who invented the Singer Sewing Machine reached an impasse when he could not get the thread to run through the needle consistently. When he was at his wit's end, he dreamed one night that he was being chased by natives carrying spears. As they came closer, he noticed that every spear had a hole at the bottom of the blade, and the next morning he made a needle with its eye near the point, instead of at the top. His machine was complete.

We, too, can profit from the unconscious abilities within us: we only need to learn how. Just as we seem to carry the memories of those who have gone before us within our minds, so we also inherit the strengths and the immunities of our great ancestors, the survivors. To rediscover those strengths, we could do worse than observe the ways of the animal kingdom: bats with their radar, dolphins with their telepathic communication, birds with their sense of navigation. What we are seeing in them is the harmonious relationship of body, conscious and unconscious minds.

If we are to survive, we need to re-create ourselves, to combine the knowledge of the present with the abilities of the past. We need to create a new mind, a mind that can understand the mysteries of regression, a mind that cannot keep secrets from itself. I believe we are on the way towards that goal; how far, we cannot tell. If not for us, then for the future, we should pursue that end. It is time we reclaimed our minds.

And finally … from Herbert Spencer again:

Opinion is ultimately determined by the feelings, and not by the intellect.

Appendix A: Ray Bryant

[Personal testimony]

Once I thought my mind to be the only really exclusive preserve I could claim to possess, the only place in the world that was absolutely my domain, my secret.

Now I am not so sure.

Now I have learned that, somehow, I share it with others long dead. Not only my memories and experiences and prejudices are lodged there, but also those of many other different people who went before me.

I have discovered this through being regressed to past lives under hypnosis – many, many times. But don't ask me how it can be, or what it is that happens to us, for I still honestly do not know.

All I do know is that, whenever I am hypnotized, I can recall the memories of a nineteenth-century Essex farm lad called Robert Sawyer, and before him a Crimean War veteran called Sergeant Reuben Stafford; before him an eighteenth-century coachman named Wilfred Anderton, before him a little girl who died at the age of eight or thereabouts, before her a seventeenth-century governess called Elizabeth and, for all I know, others yet to be discovered.

One of them, Sergeant Stafford, certainly existed. He was born in about 1824 and died by drowning in 1879. His entire army life is on record, and whenever I am questioned under hypnosis on that record, I am invariably accurate. When I was taken to the day he was wounded, at the Battle of the Sebastopol quarries in the Crimea, I again go through the agony he felt as the shrapnel struck his hand.

The other characters have not yet been proved to have lived, as Stafford has, but traces of them may be found one day.

In fact, most of the regressions I have witnessed have produced people of whom no trace can be found – but that is hardly surprising when you consider that in former ages millions of poor people passed through this life without leaving any memorial or any mark whatsoever. They were not all Marie Antoinettes, or Dick Turpins, or Napoleon Bonapartes, as some of the more fanciful 'regression' sessions produce.

I must admit that, when I first went to see hypnotist Joe Keeton back in 1981, to write a series of features on hypnosis for my newspaper, I had always been fascinated by the idea of reincarnation and was eager to have a try at 're-living' past lives. However, you soon find Joe to be a very down-to-earth character, who quickly tries to knock out of your head all imaginative notions about the supernatural.

He is by profession a hypnotherapist, and deeply interested in the ancient science of hypnosis as a practical means of reaching down to all the latent abilities the human mind holds. Regressing people is his hobby. It's a subject that fascinates him, and has done for a quarter of a century or more. He has conducted thousands of sessions and has miles of tape-recordings to show that here is a phenomenon worthy of deeper research by the universities. That is because even more wondrous than the results of the regressions are the medical benefits that apparently can be drawn from the use of hypnosis with patients suffering all sorts of supposedly incurable conditions.

Some doctors are very interested in the work of Joe Keeton and others like him. It may not be too many more years before hypnosis as a medical aid comes out of the 'fringe' category and gains a new respectability.

That is an entirely different subject, though. All I am really qualified to talk about is my own experience of hypnotic regression.

Through Joe I learned that reincarnation is not the ultimate and only possible explanation for regression to past lives. He opened my eyes to the theories of memories inherited through the genes, of telepathic communication, of cryptamnesia, in which the marvellous computer-like ability of the mind stores information acquired long ago without our being consciously aware of its retention, of perhaps a kind of cosmic memory-bank which all of us can draw on and even, as some would want to believe, a branch of spiritualism.

How is it that I can be taken back to the winter of 1855 and feel the bitter cold that Reuben Stafford felt in the Crimea, when I myself have never had to suffer such conditions? How is it that I can speak of his life, when I myself have never served in the armed forces? How is it that I can tell you precisely the days of his promotions to corporal, to sergeant, to colour-sergeant, the day of his discharge and the day of his death, when it is very unlikely that such events were ever written down anywhere except in the army and coroner's court records that I had been unaware of?

At one regression session, when I had been put through again the moment of his drowning in the Thames (apparently the suicide of a very unhappy man), the group handed me a copy of his birth certificate. That was a very strange moment, as you may imagine.

I did not feel fear, or any other disagreeable emotion, however. I only felt a kind of sadness, and then an understanding of the deep peace I, Ray Bryant, had always felt within the vicinity of water. The miserable Reuben Stafford had found peace at last in the water, and I had always subconsciously remembered it.

Later I visited the graveyard where Reuben Stafford was known to be buried. I could not find the actual grave, for unfortunately it has long since given way to other burials, but again that feeling was right. I looked at the trees there and knew that their roots touched at least a part of the dust that had been Reuben.

'Reuben,' I murmured, 'today I have brought your memories back to you. Memories and physical remains together again, for the first time in more than a hundred years.'

You see, you get very fond of these characters whose memories you discover in your mind. They are, after all, a part of your own make-up. In re-living their lives, you often discover that some of the prejudices of convictions you have always held do not really belong to you at all but were a part of their lives.

For example, I had always had an irrational dislike of the French, for no reason I could fathom. Then I was regressed to Reuben Stafford and found that he, like thousands of other British soldiers, despised their French allies in the Crimea. Since realizing that this was his prejudice and not mine, my unnecessary dislike of French people has vanished, and now at the age of forty-six I have started learning French.

So how can this marvellous phenomenon happen?

I would love to believe in reincarnation, and I have not entirely dismissed its possibility from my mind. The thought-waves are, after all, an energy force, and any scientist will tell you energy cannot be destroyed. Is it possible that this life force within us leaps from one physical being to another, from death to conception, again and again, like a spark leaping from a broken cable?

Since meeting Joe Keeton, however, I have had to give all the other theories due consideration.

Spiritualism I dismiss completely, though others may not. This is not calling up the dead from the other side, because in hypnotic regression the characters we encounter can speak only of their own times, their own memories – nothing of the present.

Genetically inherited memory is an interesting idea, but has some serious flaws. The most important to my mind are these:

a) If we are dealing here only with memories we have inherited from our ancestors, you would expect some of your known grandparents or great-grandparents, or uncles or aunts, or distant cousins, to turn up somewhere in regressions. But I have yet to meet anyone who says they have regressed to a known ancestor.

b) Again, if we are dealing with inherited memory, we should be able to regress only to people who had children. Time and time again, however, regressees produce the memories of characters who never had children. So how could they have passed on their memories through the genes?

Telepathic communication? It's certainly a possibility. In the regression groups I have attended, there is always a notable telepathic ability among the members. It would explain how some of the information could be passed on subconsciously to the person under hypnosis, but unfortunately not all, for the regressees often produce information which is then checked and found to be accurate, so it is unlikely anyone in the group passed it to him or her in the first place.

Cryptamnesia, facts the subconscious buried deeply long ago, without the conscious realizing it was doing so? A favourite theory, but too easy an answer in my view.

If you saw the episode of the Yorkshire Television series *Arthur C. Clarke's World of Strange Powers*, in which a little of my case history was included, you would have heard Arthur C. Clarke dismiss all regression cases as cryptamnesia. He produced two case histories which 'proved' his point. Joe Keeton could produce a thousand case histories which would smash the claim easily.

Certainly cryptamnesia may explain many regressions. Particularly it would explain those fanciful 'regressions' where people in a light state of hypnosis – quite honestly – believe themselves to be Charles II, Julius Caesar (usually speaking perfect English), Oliver Cromwell or Joan of Arc.

With such characters, certainly the incredible memory-bank could have stored away enough acquired information over the years to make the regression seem authentic.

But probably 99.9 per cent of the regressions conducted by Joe Keeton have produced characters who were peasants, farm workers, servants, dullards, mostly people who could not write their own names. Who ever wrote down full accounts of their miserable lives? And yet time and again at regression sessions, they 'come alive' and speak of a world only they could have known, and describe it in a way only they could have seen, felt, heard and smelt. To speak of those regressions as purely cryptamnesia is plainly nonsense.

Then what is regression, you ask me, after four years of experimentation with it?

I don't know. And anyway, you will believe what you must. I can only wonder that I, perhaps, am the only living person who can claim to have seen Florence Nightingale, in real life, in a hospital tent in the Crimea.

I have seen vast herds of buffalo on the North American plains; I have experienced drowning and wounds that were not mine; I have seen the English Civil War enacted not by the Sealed Knot Society but by people who were really there, and I have bumped and creaked and galloped and bucked with a mail coach along the rutted highways of eighteenth-century England, and I have seen a highwayman at his hanging.

That to me is the wonder of it all.

Perhaps the answers do not matter, only the delightful knowledge that our own memories of this life and all we love will never die.

I for one am no longer afraid of death. I have done it many times before.

Testimony of Colonel J.A.C. Bird, OBE

When invited by Yorkshire Television to interrogate Ray Bryant while he was being filmed under hypnosis, I willingly accepted. My instructions were to pose the sort of questions on details of the regiment's life and actions in the Crimea unlikely to have been picked up by Ray, consciously or otherwise, in the course of his lifetime. Because Ray, under hypnosis, was 'living the events' in his subconscious mind, I had to present my questions in a topical way as though I was sharing the experiences with him.

In order to eliminate as far as possible the chances of asking questions on aspects which might have been fairly widely published, I chose my material largely from letters and accounts from regimental history which to my knowledge have not been made public, certainly outside the regiment.

I questioned Ray for almost an hour on a wide range of

subjects about the campaign which required a descriptive and often detailed answer. In general he gave convincing replies accompanied by appropriate emotional responses. Some answers were surprisingly inaccurate, others astonishingly near the truth. My overall impression was that his subconscious descriptions were real and not figments of imagination or residual data from some forgotten reading of a book or article on the Crimea.

My own theory is that somehow, probably in the same way as other human characteristics are passed by birth, Ray has inherited memories of Sergeant Stafford rather like a tape. In this context, I was impressed with his authenticity and honesty.

Appendix B: Marjorie Bunyard

[Marjorie Bunyard BDS LDS PhD is Emeritus Senior Lecturer at Liverpool School of Dental Surgery. Personal testimony.]

Dental surgeons are much concerned with relief of pain. Toothache is known to all people, and there is archaeological evidence that it was known to our primitive ancestors.

Anaesthesia is a relatively recent invention and, in spite of advances in local anaesthesia, many people are still apprehensive about having dental treatment and put off visits to the dentist. It is not uncommon for dentists to find patients who feel they have to have tranquillizers before a visit, and there are a few people who ask for a general anaesthetic even to have fillings.

I have been interested in the use of hypnotherapy to allay fear and reduce perception of pain since my student days. Although I had attended weekend courses in the medical and dental use of hypnosis, and knew there were many excellent practitioners in the UK, I felt that the technique deserves better recognition from both dentists and doctors.

After seeing Joe Keeton in a BBC programme in November 1979 about regression, I was convinced that his ability was far better than anything I had seen previously. I was pleased to find that he lived only ten miles away from me on Merseyside. He invited me to attend the experimental group sessions at his home every fortnight during the spring of 1980, where I was fascinated to observe the phenomenon that takes place during deep hypnosis that is described as regression. I cannot contribute anything new to the discussion about whether this is reincarnation, cryptamnesia, entry into the cosmic consciousness or any other theories. I can say with total conviction that the subjects are not cheating or acting and are amazingly consistent in their behaviour, while apparently in the part of another character or personality. Joe himself makes it clear that he has no tendency towards any of the theories, but simply says, 'It happens', and invites anyone to observe it and try to find an explanation.

Although the dramatic phenomenon of regression makes good television-programme material, there are several peripheral effects and benefits that are received freely by all the people who are subjects. It is not necessary to know the reason or explanation of these effects to take advantage of them, just as we can use an aspirin as a painkiller without knowing how it works.

It was obvious that many of the subjects had originally visited Joe Keeton because of physical complaints, such as pain due to migraine or chronic rheumatism, or nightmares, drug dependency, back ache and many other discomforts that are not capable of relief by direct and definite medical treatment, the sort of things that we tend to think we have to 'learn to live with'. The subjects had usually gone to visit Joe Keeton after being referred by a medical practitioner or by recommendation from another cured patient.

Joe Keeton's method is to teach the subject, usually within an hour, how to accept that the hypnotic state is totally within the subject's own control, that it is effectively self-hypnosis and that, once it is recognized, the state can be entered into at will. After being guided a few times, the subject is given a verbal formula to use to become relaxed, taught how to time the hypnotic state accurately from a few minutes to a whole night's sleep, and told to practise at least twice a day until it becomes habit. While doing this, the subject learns immediately that the perception of pain, once it has served its purpose of drawing attention to something wrong with the body, can be turned off. For the future, the subject recognizes that the pain warning of something as real as a broken arm is a signal that he must get proper medical attention. But once the fracture is set and the limb immobilized in plaster, the pain warning is superfluous and, with deep relaxation, the patient can reduce the pain perception without the use of drugs.

I had suffered from severe attacks of headache, of the type

described as migraine, at intervals of seven or eight weeks for several years. I had all the classical symptoms of flashing lights, blurred vision, severe one-sided pain lasting for as much as two days, with vomiting and inability to tolerate light. My left eyelid swelled and my eye watered so that I was hardly able to see. I had tried all the various pain-relievers offered for migraine, the very multiplicity of remedies underlining the fact that treatment is difficult. After seeing Joe Keeton's demonstration of control of pain, the next time I saw flashing lights and knew I was in for two days of being incapacitated with pain, I went to see him.

Within twenty minutes he had me in a state of hypnosis and showed me how to do it for myself. The pain of the headache disappeared immediately and has never returned in the form of migraine. Six years later, I have never had an attack of migraine. I have only once had even a slight headache, and that was when I had an upper respiratory infection and probably had sinusitis, but even that pain was relieved by self-hypnosis.

Although my primary reason for asking Joe Keeton to teach me hypnosis was that I had the pain of migraine, at the same time I had some arthritis of my finger joint – my fingers being rather painful, difficult to bend and so swollen that I had recently had to have my wedding ring cut to remove it. While I was hypnotized at that first session, Joe Keeton told me to bend my fingers into fists, and then told me to wake up and look at them. I did as he asked, and can remember the complete astonishment when I saw my fingers bent completely, as I had not been able to do that for months. By the next day, all swelling from my fingers and wrists had gone completely, and it has not returned. I tried to rationalize that by telling myself that the swelling was dispelled because I was moving the fingers and not feeling any pain, but in fact no explanation or reason is necessary when results are so rapidly self-evident and permanent. There is an obvious application for this in the field of physiotherapy.

Shortly after this, I asked if I could bring dental students to see him, both in order to learn how hypnosis can be brought about and to decide if they wanted to know more about it in order to help their patients when they were qualified. About fifty students and dental colleagues went in groups of about ten. Those who volunteered to be subjects for demonstration received the benefit of finding out how to relieve the discomfort of their own aches and pains, and learned relaxation. Naturally dental students are very interested in pain relief and in helping their patients overcome apprehension.

In addition to that, they were interested in another facet of the hypnotic state that may be more nearly related to the phenomenon of access to the unconscious mind that is manifested in the experiments with regression. The training to be a dentist is a long and difficult one and involves committing to memory a heavy load of facts, to be tested in oral and written examinations for which students work long hours. We all know about those tricks of memory when we try and fail to remember something, and say it is 'on the tip of the tongue', and have to wait for it to surface spontaneously later, when we have stopped trying to remember it. In the self-induced hypnotic state, it becomes incredibly easy to recall at will all those bits of information which are buried for most of the time. Most agree that in the unconscious we retain the memory of everything that has ever happened to us, including details of early memories.

Whether learning a language or studying for examinations, the ability of instant recall is greatly enhanced by the use of hypnotherapy. I am certain that those students who learned the technique of self-hypnosis for their own benefit became much more confident about their ability to learn new facts and to remember them at will under the stress of examinations.

I remember two students in particular. One, Brian, was an older student, coming to university at the age of thirty, after a laboratory job, and hampered by his belief that he could not learn as easily as he could when he was at school. He had failed the twenty-minute oral examination in biochemistry and said that his mind had 'just gone blank', although he had worked hard and remembered the answers after the examination, but too late. He went to see Joe Keeton three days before repeating the examination and, while in hypnosis, was convinced that everything he had learned was indeed remembered and could be recalled completely when he was asked questions by the examiners. He then passed the examination without difficulty and, fortunately, overcame his nervousness about oral examinations for the rest of his course.

The other was a young woman, Janet, who in her final year had a sports accident so that she had a fractured pelvis and one leg with four fractures. She had been one of Joe Keeton's volunteer subjects a month previously and had learned pain-control, among other things. When I heard of the accident, I thought she would probably have to postpone her final examination, only five months off. We were delighted, but surprised, when she came back to work in the clinic less than three weeks later, on crutches with a leg in plaster up to the hips. She was incredibly cheerful and told me that, when she had the accident, she remained conscious and in very great pain until she was in the accident ward of the hospital. She then told herself that, as the doctors and nurses were there and taking care of her, she did not have to put up with the pain any longer, so she just put herself into a state of hypnosis, so relaxed that the casualty officer was alarmed and thought she had collapsed. Although she felt some pain later, she was able to use self-hypnosis to get to sleep and was able to avoid taking drugs. She completed her training without interruption, showing great courage.

From my own experience with hypnotherapy to cure migraine and arthritis, and as a patient myself in the dental chair, where I put myself to sleep for the duration of whatever treatment I need, I would strongly recommend the use of hypnosis in dentistry.

Appendix C: Brian Hitchen

[Brian Hitchen, Editor of *The Star*. Personal testimony.]

When Joe Keeton and I met for the first time on a rainy night in April 1980, he didn't like me and I didn't like him. So what happened in the hours that followed had absolutely nothing to do with empathy, sentiment or faith.

I had come from London to see Joe to arrange a major feature on regression for *Now!* magazine, based on the book *Encounters with the Past*. The journey, in a hired Hertz car from Manchester airport, had been through sleet and driving rain. When I banged on the enormous knocker of Joe's rambling red-brick Victorian house in the Wirral, a rather snooty suburb of Liverpool, I was greeted by a figure of Orson Wells-like proportions.

'You are late and dinner is about to be served,' he thundered. The meal – two-inch-thick porterhouse steaks accompanied by excellent wine – was an uneasy affair. Joe felt that, like many journalists of the past, I had come to do a hatchet job on him. In fact, I was totally open-minded about him and his work. But he was nasty and aggressive, and I kept wondering why, as a senior executive of a prestigious news magazine, I had bothered to come myself when I could just as easily have sent somebody else. Only his delightful and very attractive Titian-haired wife, Monica, made the meal bearable.

We discussed the book and its contents at length. What made Joe Keeton's regressions different from and far more credible than any other hypnotist's was that the people he regressed did not come through as highwaymen, Napoleon or Henry VIII in previous lives, but as ordinary people. They paraded through his tape-recorded sessions of regressions as simple creatures out of another age. They were sailors' wives, clergymen's daughters, a captain of a Liverpool slaver and even a Victorian street urchin who was murdered in the cellar of the Liverpool slum where she spent her short, pathetic life which ended in a spine-chilling scream.

We sat and talked far into the night in the panelled study, with its sound equipment and reel-to-reel tape decks where Joe practised his art with the patience of a Jesuit priest.

Over glasses of whisky, Joe Keeton told me of his skill with hypnosis and his ability to unlock the most frozen minds. I already knew of his work with the police and of the documented occasions on which he had been able to help by 're-running' the memories of victims so that even in the split second before the impact of an accident they were able, under Joe's gentle persuasion, to remember registration numbers, or fractions of them.

Around one o'clock in the morning, when Joe had perhaps decided that I wasn't as bad as he expected, he made what I thought to be a preposterous claim. He said he could cure arthritis.

For two years I had suffered agonies with an arthritic little finger on my right hand. The disease was so advanced that the right-hand pinkie looked like a swollen chipolata and in winter often turned the most disturbing shade of purple. When I shook hands, pain shot up my arm, and for most of the time the finger was crooked at the first joint and always looked angry.

I remember as if it was yesterday when I stuck out my hand and said to Joe: 'I have arthritis. Could you cure me?'

He shifted his then twenty-stone bulk in his big black leather armchair, leaned forward and took my hand.

There was no mumbo-jumbo, no staring into my eyes or swinging watch chains. He simply felt the joints of my little finger and said, 'Yes, there are lots of crystals here. No doubt at all it's arthritis. But you won't have any more trouble with it. In a couple of hours it will be gone.'

With that he let go of my hand, poured a last nightcap for the pair of us and then ushered me off to bed in the guest-room.

When I came down for breakfast the next morning, Joe was busily building a magnificent kedgeree in the kitchen. 'How's your finger?' he asked. I looked, and for the first time in two years my right hand was perfectly normal. The joints on my little finger were no longer swollen, no longer crippled into a pyramid position.

'Jesus Christ,' I said. 'I don't believe it.'

To which he grinned and said: 'You haven't got much option. It looks to me as though your arthritis has gone away, and it won't be coming back either.'

Joe Keeton never tells anyone he is a faith healer, and nor is he. I do not think that even he knows how he does it. But he certainly did it for me! His view is that, if somebody is religious and after a healing session wants to go home and say a prayer, well, that's all right by him. But it certainly isn't anything to do with faith.

His philosophy is really rather simplistic and I have never been able to find a hole in his argument.

Joe says that all cures in bodily ailments are contained in the mind. When the body is cut, signals go from the brain to the injured area with a chemical cipher giving it instructions to cure itself. In this way the blood clots and within forty-eight hours tissues have healed and knitted together. When cells become corrupted and the body fails to isolate and reject them, it is, according to Joe, simply because the body's printed circuit has gone wrong. The circuit is jammed and healing signals are blocked. Joe believes, and I have absolutely no reason to doubt him, that the mind can be persuaded to remember the healing recipes and despatch the signals to the right part of the body.

Over the weeks I spent on and off in the Wirral conducting the serialization of the book that featured Joe, I sat in at several of his healing sessions. They were successful at usually the first, and always the second, attempt. But sometimes they were touched by laughter as well.

I remember one evening a pretty nurse in her late twenties arriving somewhat shyly at the house with a colleague of a similar age. She complained that she had a squeak and clicking sound coming from her right kneecap.

Joe relaxed her with his deep brown voice and then told her that her problems were over and that the clicking would bother her no longer. When he brought her back to full consciousness, because on this occasion he had put her under slight hypnosis, she asked if she might visit the bathroom. He told her that the stairs would be a magnificent opportunity to test her 'new' knee, and off she went.

A few minutes later she called from the stairs and said something funny had happened. Several of us, including Joe, hurried into the black-and-white tiled hall outside his study and watched as the nurse walked downstairs.

She giggled; 'The clicking has gone from my right knee, but it is coming from the left!' We listened – and it was.

'I think you had better come back next week,' Joe said.

And my finger? Five years later it is still perfectly all right, and I shake hands without feeling as though 20,000 volts are shooting up my arm. But don't ask me how he did it.

Joe Keeton is, in my opinion, a magician. And we are still very good friends.

Index

All names given inside quotation marks refer to characters revealed under past-life regression.